ETHICAL RELIGION
◄——— *and* ———►
CHRISTIAN ACTIVISM

*A Handbook for the
Modern Christian Making
Church Life Meaningful*

JOHN SHELLENBERGER

ETHICAL RELIGION AND CHRISTIAN ACTIVISM
A HANDBOOK FOR THE MODERN CHRISTIAN
MAKING CHURCH LIFE MEANINGFUL

iUniverse books may be ordered through booksellers or by contacting:

iUniverse
1663 Liberty Drive
Bloomington, IN 47403
www.iuniverse.com
844-349-9409

Because of the dynamic nature of the Internet, any web addresses or links contained in this book may have changed since publication and may no longer be valid. The views expressed in this work are solely those of the author and do not necessarily reflect the views of the publisher, and the publisher hereby disclaims any responsibility for them.

Any people depicted in stock imagery provided by Getty Images are models, and such images are being used for illustrative purposes only.
Certain stock imagery © Getty Images.

Scripture quotations marked RSV are taken from the Revised Standard Version of the Bible, copyright © 1946, 1952, 1971 by the Division of Christian Education of the National Council of the Churches of Christ in the USA. Used by permission.

ISBN: 978-1-5320-9702-7 (sc)
ISBN: 978-1-5320-9704-1 (hc)
ISBN: 978-1-5320-9703-4 (e)

Library of Congress Control Number: 2020917040

Print information available on the last page.

iUniverse rev. date: 10/13/2020

CONTENTS

INTRODUCTION

This is a book for thoughtful people who frequently attend church and are potential or active church members. It is an effort to bring religion, and specifically Christianity, into the 21st century, devoid of the super-naturalistic creeds and beliefs of the past 2000 years. Yet, it honors devotion to the past and to the person and teachings of Jesus of Nazareth, the progenitor of the faith we embrace.

If you grew up in a church-going family and had a Sunday School education, you probably absorbed certain information, ideas and practices that have carried you into adulthood. Many of us had life-changing experiences at church camp during the summer and these experiences are remembered with fondness.

In college, you found it necessary to ignore or by-pass the challenges posed to your faith, so you continued on with a dualistic sense of what you knew and believed. Unfortunately, the religious or faith aspect of your belief system failed to keep pace with your more scientific or rational belief system. It is time to change that.

This is not a treatise against God. It is a plea for adhering to a God who gives us a standard for morality and ethical behavior. It is not a tirade against Christianity but an argument for adhering to a true and just and, intelligent and righteous Christianity. This is a protest against the hypocritical façade of evangelical Christianity and a focus on the passion Jesus had for living an affirmative life devoted to others. It is a call to common sense, not an impassioned plea for mindless affirmations of senseless things. It is a summons to true faith and confidence, not in charlatans, but in your own conscious resources.

1

THE RELIGIOUS CHALLENGE
IN THE MODERN WORLD

THE CHALLENGE OF LIVING TODAY

For thousands of years, the human experience was vastly different from the world in which we live today. People lived without instant communication devices, with extremely limited health care, without the ability to travel very far from home, without work-saving appliances, in fairly primitive and even unhealthy conditions, with little public influence and without access to anything other than local information. Most people were illiterate, uneducated and poorly informed. People survived at the mercy of the elements of nature. They worshipped and adopted ritualistic practices among themselves in order to survive.

In the modern developed world, most of these conditions have changed dramatically and humans have control of most of the problems of human survival. We know more, we travel more, we communicate immeasurably better with anyplace in the world, we are healthier and live much longer, and we work more efficiently and successfully. At our fingertips is technology that former generations could not even imagine, let alone implement and utilize.

Still, we are confronted by enormous problems, not only in the world but in our personal lives as well. We are confronted with innumerable decisions, with an overabundance of information, with time-consuming challenges, with sophisticated social mores and practices, with the knowledge that challenges our most cherished beliefs.

Among those challenges is the need to integrate our inherited belief systems into a world of scientific, technical and cultural knowledge that has developed at an ever-quickening and sophisticated pace. Regardless of our culture, we have tried to hold on to those religious ideas that have been passed on through the generations. Too often, those religious beliefs have failed to keep up with the challenges of a modern human culture and are becoming increasingly irrelevant to our daily lives.

RELIGION AS ENTERTAINMENT

A segment of society looks to its church and church experience for its entertainment. Turn on your television set at night after ten and you'll see everything from "Christian Rock" to a maudlin movie to an emotional soul singer to an enthusiastic revival to a tour of Jerusalem and you'll see what the choices are for anyone who is seeking that kind of entertainment. The justification for that is that the programming is what brings 'em in. As Marshall McLuhan preached: "The medium is the message".

Churches have always been centers of the arts: in paintings, in sculpture, in music, even in dance and dramatic performance – the best in each of those arenas to lift the spirit and challenge the soul – to supplement and enhance the other elements of worship and soul searching. Perhaps it has always been, but more recently, quality has been sacrificed for entertainment – and people are attracted to church for its emotional appeal alone.

It's a human desire to want to be entertained. It has been happening since the dawn of history – and now it has become very sophisticated with the high tech media that is currently available. Of course, there is nothing wrong with wanting to be entertained – or with the entertainment itself – but one should not think that the entertainment itself is what Christianity is all about. Jesus did not travel about in order to entertain but to lead followers on a more righteous and meaningful path for living. Regardless of the type of music and regardless of the emotional feelings that are evoked, this is not what it is all about – and it wouldn't be a bad idea to acknowledge that what we are called to do is a far cry from being entertained.

ARE TV EVANGELISTS A SOCIAL ASSET?

Every night on television, competing with the several night show hosts, there is a spate of TV evangelists who spout messages that are unrelated to the real world. Jimmy Swaggart shouts "Hallelujah", his son Danny talks about the future as though the Book of Revelation has it precisely laid out, T.D. Jakes cajoles his congregants to part with their money, Joel Osteen does cartwheels to make everyone feel good, and Jim Bakker will sell you a package of emergency health food so you can survive the Last Judgment. These people are con artists and grifters.

What these purveyors of wisdom provide is a message that then appeals to their listeners but that is unconnected to reality and is not only intellectually lazy but that is untruthful as well. There are those for whom the message brings them out of their misery and isolation. It fills a void in their emotional lives and helps them to bring the disjointed pieces of their lives back together. At the same time, it leads them into an unreality that has nothing to do with a discovery of the truth and a recognition of the complexity of life.

THE CHURCH AS AN INSTITUTION FOR SOCIALIZING

For many people, the church fills a social need – and that is the primary reason for their affiliation with it. It is a place for being with people who share some common traits and interests. The belief system is only incidental to the primary goal of socializing with friends and acquaintances. That's not a message that clergy want to hear – but it's a reality for most people. Since people prefer to associate with others of their same social characteristics, different churches in a community are usually characterized by racial, class and income distinctions. A recent *New York Times* article indicated that Presbyterians and Episcopalians tend to be the most affluent of Protestant groups while Pentecostals and Baptists tend to be among the lowest income groups. The same distinction applies to educational level.

Suggesting again that church activity is primarily centered around socializing rather than a focused dedication to resolving social issues, note that it is easier to get people to participate in staging a spaghetti dinner at the church than it is to perform the more compassionate work of teaching or counseling low income individuals or families in a community. Bible study groups tend to be social gatherings, discussing homespun gossip after fifteen minutes discussing an obscure Bible passage rather than talking about more controversial ethical issues. The Bible passage is often unrelated to the other discussion.

In past years, when the world was more of an agricultural society, church attendance was a primary way of bringing people and families together on a regular basis so that they could share information and chat among one another. People would spend all day Sunday together in worship, then eating and planning and doing other activities, concluding with another worship service in the evening. As communities urbanized, mobility increased and other forms of entertainment and socializing came on the scene, church activity diminished and narrowed to a Sunday morning service and perhaps an evening youth program.

So, if church participation primarily fulfills a need for socialization, what does that do to the church's theology and belief commitment? Just how irrelevant is it? To what extent should it be regarded as true and important in human life?

THE ROLE AND RESPONSIBILITY
OF A RELIGIOUS PERSPECTIVE

For all of human history, mysteries were explained in a supernatural way. Gradually, over the recent past, we have begun to find rational explanations for many of these mysteries and, in the process, whittled away at the supernatural explanations. In the twentieth century, and now in the twenty-first, we have discarded many of the superstitions and non-natural beliefs of the past. In Jesus' day, it was commonly accepted that there were miraculous things that would and did happen - and, they were reported as such. Today, the realm of the miraculous has been narrowed down but not totally dissipated. Nonetheless, it is our perspective that everything has a natural or rational explanation, even though we may not fully understand it yet. Thus, supernatural explanations are no longer sufficient for our understanding.

We have discarded the superstitions and spirits of the past and accepted scientific and rational explanations for things that are difficult to understand. And, yet, we are still asked in our churches to accept the miraculous: concepts such as Virgin birth, turning water into wine, the resurrection of the dead (whether it is Lazarus or Jesus), walking on water, the Holy Spirit, the curing of the blind, the Transfiguration, eternal life and the efficacy of prayer. A segment of the Christian world believes in modern curative miracles, the beatification of "saints", and the transformation of wine into the blood of Christ.

Looking back to Jesus' time, we need to reinterpret the "miracles". Whatever happened, the curing of the sick, the walking on water, the changing of water into wine, these all have natural explanations – and were reinterpreted by the Gospel writers over time from extraordinary acts into miracles. That was the mindset in pre-modern times. It is no longer sufficient. Even in his time (the eighteenth century), Thomas Jefferson was so hostile to the idea of miracles that he published an edition of the Gospels that excluded the miracles. We need to understand these events in modern terms and be aware of what Jesus was really about and what he was trying to accomplish.

For many of us, we were born into a family and circle of friends where it was the accepted norm that you would adopt the beliefs and practices of the group. You would learn the catechism, recite the creeds, attend the services and engage in the frivolous things centered upon the church, perhaps even some worthy projects intended to help others. Even without any evidence, you were expected to acknowledge the truth of the Bible and the professions of faith that attended it. In fact, you were expected to believe a certain interpretation of the Bible and of its various books that modern knowledge would challenge – but you weren't encouraged to understand these multiple interpretations.

So, forget about what you have learned or been told. Think of your mind as a blank slate upon which thoughts and ideas are etched from infancy, some true, some questionable, some we know now to be just plain false. How do you know what is taught to you is true? Many teachings, traditions and assumptions, whether in primitive villages or in the modern city, are inaccurate, misinformed, misinterpreted or misunderstood.

Just suppose you grew up in a forest without parents or tutors or instruction of any kind, only with the attention of animals who brought you food. You would regard them as your parents and brothers and sisters. They might look different than you, but they would also have some similarities: eyes, ears, nose, mouth, four appendages, even genital and anal organs. They would need food (like you) and breathe air, and drink water. If you could see their internal organs, they would be like yours: stomach, intestines, heart, gall bladder, liver, kidneys, muscle, etc. They would bleed red blood (like you) and salivate and carry on similar bodily functions. They would even share in emotions, like happiness, contentment, curiosity, sadness, annoyance, anger, even hatred. In some way, they must be related to you. You are one of them. You are an animal. Some are herbivorous, some are carnivorous, some are omnivorous, just like you. They die; you die. There are many animals that are different in appearance but share the same bodily organs and functions. What makes you think you are different?

We now know that humans, for hundreds of thousands of years, lived lives that were very much like other animals. Perhaps several hundred thousand years ago, they began to fashion tools for use in hunting and, later, cultivating. They began to do things that were qualitatively a giant step above other animals. But, they were still animals. They cooperated in certain endeavors (so do wolves), they argued (so do chimpanzees); they relied on one another (so do ungulates); they fought with one another (as do mountain goats); they mourned their dead (as do elephants).

There are animals that engage in certain rituals: courting rituals, food rituals, communication rituals, death rituals. Humans began to develop more sophisticated rituals that gradually developed into religious ceremonies and posited a spirit world in which they could participate. Humans began to think of themselves as different from the rest of the animal kingdom. They were in relationship with the gods and eventually with God. Theological concepts developed from a very primitive form to a more sophisticated monotheism.

They lived in a world of darkness, with the dark only being penetrated from the light of torches. The darkness meant the unknown, the dangerous, the evil. They conjured the forces of darkness that could only be countered by the forces of light. From that condition, they developed a primitive belief system that gradually evolved over time. But, there are still those who believe in more primitive religious concepts: spirits who control events, images that bleed, ghosts who wander among their familiar haunts, gods who intervene in natural cataclysms and human lives. We still pray for God's intervention to restore a dying person to heath.

How is it possible for a God to intervene in a human life in any significant way when millions of people were allowed to perish under Stalin, Hitler, Saddam Hussein and their genocidal predecessors (and successors), despite the prayers of many? If you have ever thanked God for saving you from a terrible tragedy, what about those who perished? Why didn't God save them as well?

If you peruse the back channels on your television set in the evening, you will find all kinds of religious programming – from the dull and dreary to the exuberant and thrilling, from the authoritarian guru to the on-site harbinger of immediate doom, from the Christian rock performing band to the traditional Mass, from the mystic healer to the syrupy sentimentalist. What they all have in common is that they are intended to meet a certain emotional need that differs from person to person, to entertain, albeit to those seeking different forms of entertainment. Each in its own way is intended to draw you in rather than to send you out. And, each wants you to contribute money for your entertainment.

Perhaps we could identify some standards for what a religious perspective should do in the world – a perspective that will make its existence worthwhile and make this a better world and us a better people. Perhaps those criteria should be something like the following:

> Encourage the compassionate side of our personhood;
> Make us more sensitive to the needs of others;
> Make us more passionate about justice for others;
> Help us to be better and more meaningfully connected to one another;
> Help us to be more self-confident;
> Help us to realize our potential more fully;
> Encourage human creativity;
> Contribute to peace;
> Make us more eager to learn;
> Improve our capacity for understanding and knowledge;
> Make us more truthful and honest;
> Make us less focused upon and dependent on money & its acquisition;
> Make us more aware of the deeper underlying meanings of life.

What is the role and responsibility of a religious perspective? Why be devoted to anything at all?

There is no necessarily objective reason to embrace a religious perspective – except for one's choice to do so – in order to, in some way, become a better person by fulfilling some purpose. Different people see life in different ways – and see themselves as having different goals. In the recent past, we have seen the actions of people who see their purpose as being destructive and taking the lives of others in the process. In contrast to that, some people are willing to sacrifice themselves in order to save others – or to benefit others.

What has been most interesting are the efforts to turn would-be terrorists around and help them to see a positive purpose in living. If anything, that is what a religious perspective is. It's certainly what is a Christian perspective on human existence. It's the process of redemption and restoration.

THE EFFORT OF THE CHURCH TO MODERNIZE

This is not the first time the church has sought to "modernize", to be more relevant and interactive with the time in which it finds itself. It has, in fact, attempted to do so across the years. The church's recent efforts to "modernize" in this country have shown a more auditorium-like gathering place (as opposed to the traditional church sanctuary), video projections and rock bands and a contemporary musical idiom. Sermons are more message-like and are even read from teleprompters. Churches sponsor foot & bicycle races, have baseball teams, sponsor fund-raising booths at county fairs, build gymnasiums and operate private schools.

FINDING A STANDARD FOR CHURCH MEMBERS

Churches are pervasive throughout America. Every community is home to at least one, and probably several, congregations and church buildings. Church communities already exist and have the potential to become, as Paul put it, "agents of reconciliation" rather than agents of division and hostility as they have too often become. Is it possible for churches to become centers of discussion where controversy becomes the norm but without hostility?

Perhaps it is not important whether one believe in God. God's existence doesn't depend on whether we believe God exists. What's important is whether God believes in us. Are we living as though God exists and expects us to lead God fearing (ethical) lives.?

If Jesus of Nazareth is regarded as our ethical center, we have a reference point for discussing controversial issues. What becomes important is how Jesus is regarded with respect to the meaning of his life and teaching for any particular issue. Take the issue of abortion and freedom-to-choose as an example. It's not so easy to determine if Jesus would advocate for the unborn child OR for the distraught, impoverished, hopeless young woman. But, in discussing the issue, those who champion each side of the question must have respect for the ethical integrity of the other and the difficulty of finding a valid answer. It is the reference to Jesus that is crucial, reminding ourselves that he was no dogmatist.

TRUTH

Truth has recently become an endangered commodity with the President of the United States being cited by Politifact with false or mostly false assertions most of the time. Despite overwhelming evidence and agreement among the vast majority of scientists, climate change and the evolution of life are still doubted by a large percentage of the population. Polls and surveys indicate that large numbers of people believe material that is demonstrably untrue. Is the church – and are church leaders – at least partly responsible for promulgating untruths? If so, that has to change!

2

FOLLOWING JESUS

Everyone has his/her own mental image of Jesus. For some, he was/is a Superman type of hero. For others, he is a "sweet-voiced" story teller. For some, he is a strict guardian of morality. For others, he is a kindly neighbor. Some think of him primarily as the Sacrificial Lamb who has paid the price for the sins of those who believe in him. Some think of him as a Realist while some regard him as unrelated to reality. We have only a scant picture of who he really was. In the Gospels, we have short abbreviated biographies. The tendency is to make Jesus into the figure we want him to be.

For some time now (since at least the late 19th century), theologians have sought the Historical Jesus – but that search remains, for the most part, unfulfilled. The picture drawn by the Gospel writers is incomplete, leaving innumerable questions unanswered – and there are no other legitimate resources. The Nativity stories differ from one another. We know nothing about his childhood and only one incident – the visit to the Temple – during his teen age years. It is assumed that, as a young man, he worked with his father as a carpenter – but that is really an unknown period in his life. Was he schooled? Was he literate? What were his real concerns? He suddenly appears as an itinerant preacher/ teacher when he is about 30 - but the period of his ministry that is covered by the Gospels is unknown. Little is said about his family and his wandering travels are little understood. What prompted him to go on the road, teaching and preaching? How did he and his disciples feed themselves? Where did they stay at night? Was there interaction with Herod and the Roman authorities during the period of his ministry? What was the dynamic shift that prompted crowds to throw palm branches and adore him on Palm Sunday and then to reject him later in the final days of his life? There is too much about his life that we do NOT know.

No doubt, Jesus had a tremendous impact on his followers and others around him. After the Crucifixion, they couldn't let go of him. They continued to gather together and tell stories about him, even to others outside of their group. However, internally there was a group cohesion that prompted them to share together what they had (Acts 4:32). But, even in the early days, there were interpretations of Jesus wherein leaders of small groups developed their own aberrational ideas that deviated from the "mainstream": Gnostics, Montanists, Docetists and others, streams that were ultimately defeated by the more orthodox church leaders. Still, the "mainstream" had to contend with the issue of whether Jesus was in some way a divine manifestation or merely human. To say that the "orthodox" resolution which we know today was better than that of the Docetists or Montanists is problematic. All of those interpretations go beyond contending that Jesus was merely human.

The image we have of Jesus has changed through the ages. Apart from the Gospels, we have no other independent first-hand accounts of his presence in Palestine. Even taking the Gospels into account, we have no contemporaneous accounts by anyone who knew him. None of the Gospel writers knew Jesus so we only have their second-hand accounts. Early Christians saw him as a Savior from the myths of paganism. He was adorned with a halo by Medieval artists and medievalists saw him as the one who snatched them from the fires of hell.

During the Medieval era, there were stories that were created and passed around about Jesus' childhood and teen-age years. Most of those stories give him extraordinary and magical powers – though few, if any, were about his teachings and ethical judgments. What developed among the common people were ideas about sin, Purgatory, the powers of religious icons, penance, Heaven and Hell, faithful church participation, etc., the very things that Jesus dismissed or spent little time discussing, assuming the Gospels are a good record of his ministerial period and are faithful to what he talked about.

Jesus is a role model for Christians to follow, perhaps the finest role model we can think of. The Gospels portray him as humble in his associations with others – though not timid about expressing himself when he saw injustice, dishonesty and oppression. He was admired and respected by his followers, even though they were rough, uneducated and tough. He was supportive of the downtrodden and weak and caring of those who were in need. He was contemptuous of the judgmental and those who arrogantly wielded their authority, even religious officials. And, he taught, often in parables, to try to influence people with common sense ideas. His was a basic humanity in a relatively simple society. His was a world where the population was limited and stable. It was devoid of the instantaneous worldwide communications of the 21st century. It existed without the global mobility, medical technology, industrial capacity and longevity, energy consumption and enormous firepower that we must deal with today.

So, who was Jesus? In point of fact, compared with biographies of people such as Alexander the Great, Julius Caesar, Martin Luther, Galileo, Washington and Lincoln, we know precious little about him. Apart from a reference by Josephus, who was partially contemporary with him, the only information we have is from the Gospel writers, and their portraits are not first hand, with Mark being the first Gospel written about thirty years after the Crucifixion of Jesus. John is the latest Gospel written and his account is largely different from the authors of the first three Gospels, probably written about sixty years after the Crucifixion. We can dismiss John as not being very authoritative and concentrate on the three Synoptic Gospels which have many common passages among them, largely taken from two traditions, M(ark) and Q(uelle).

Assuming we can trust the essence of these Gospels, particularly the commonalities, this is what we can conclude about Jesus:

- He was an itinerant preacher and teacher in Palestine, largely in Galilee, north of Jerusalem.
- He had no possessions and lived on the generosity of others.
- He knew the Scriptures – and the law – and the teachings of the prophets.
- He taught in parables.
- He had a keen sense of what was right and wrong, attuned to what we would today call ethics.
- He valued truth and honesty.
- He was incensed by injustice and hypocrisy.
- He defended the humanity and dignity of women.
- He defended the poor, the despised and the outcast.
- He was contemptuous of the Temple authorities and Pharisees.
- He expected the end of the Age before long.
- He attended to the sick, the blind, the lame, healing some of them, perhaps with psychological means.
- His image of God was as a compassionate deity as reflected in his dealings with those who were disregarded by his society.
- His interpretation of the Law of Moses was flexible and not doctrinaire.
- He doubted that wealth was a mark of what was important.
- He was humble and did not aspire to popularity, power or greatness.
- He inspired his followers.

What happened, of course, is that his followers made him into a godlike creature of their own desire. His healings were transformed into miracles. His actions were exaggerated into supernatural events. His persona was accorded divinity status. He was given a Virgin Birth and the adoration of the Magi. He was given a genealogy, dating back to the time of Abraham (genealogies that are somewhat different in Matthew and Luke). He was accorded a Temptation with the forces of evil (the devil). These were all things that it was impossible to know by the people who wrote them. (e.g. Who recorded what was said to Mary in the Annunciation?)

In trying to understand Jesus and the words he spoke (as recorded by the Gospel writers), it helps to know something about the social milieu and context in which he appeared. It was a patriarchal society in which slavery was the accepted norm (although in the way it was practiced differed locally) and where there was a contentious history between Jew and Greek, where the Roman authority now ruled but where the locally-despised Jewish Herods now provided governmental administration. There were Jewish Zealots who were restless to overthrow all outside interference but were powerless to do much about it. When Jesus speaks, this is his context – and he often speaks guardedly, knowing about the political and social undercurrents under which the people lived. (For an excellent discussion of the social attitudes of this time & place, See *The Forgotten Creed* by Stephen J. Patterson).

Jesus and his followers were people of their time and place – and the Biblical accounts reflect those circumstances. He spoke to the issues that were then current and objected to those practices that he considered unjust. The scope of his concern was immediate and not historical or widespread. He could have inveighed against the slaughters perpetrated by King David and he could have incited violence against the Emperor in Rome. Still, he objected to the exploitative practices of the Temple moneychangers and he confronted those who would have stoned a woman for her adultery. The injustices of the Herodians and the Romans were objectionable to him and he sought to defend the defenseless against them.

If Jesus were a 21st century man, in a terribly diverse complex society and world, we can only surmise what he would have taught and represented, how he would have dealt with the difficult contemporary problems that confront us today. That is why we must be in conversation with ourselves, as well with other thoughtful peers, to try to find ethical answers to today's problems.

And, yet, he is a role model who commands our attention. Having grown up in our Western society and learned the relational values of Christian faith, it is incumbent on us as individuals to seek collective answers to the issues that confront us.

Jesus: What he thought about Human Destiny

Jesus frequently talked about the nearness of the Day of Judgment and the Kingdom of God. We usually think of the warnings as Jesus expecting an immanent Parousia – or end of time. Some scholars believe that Jesus expected an end game such as is described in the Book of Revelation as envisioned by John on the Island of Patmos. Others believe Jesus' used the concept of the Kingdom, or of the Parousia, to warn people to get their lives in order and their priorities straight before their lives were complete. Certainly, the idea of the Eschaton prevailed in the early church. No doubt, the gospel writers owe support to this first view in their accounts of the teachings and message of Jesus.

Jesus: Liberal or Conservative

To try to interpret Jesus in social or political terms that are familiar with us today is hardly useful. The conservative demeanor is to resist change and to preserve the social themes that have been inherited from the past and that provide security and comfort for the people. The liberal attitude is to make improvements that, though they may be disruptive, have the intent of improving living conditions for the greatest number of people. Jesus could be thought of as representing both approaches to society. While he seemed to revere the religious traditions of the past, he was also forward-looking in wanting to make people more sensitive to and responsive to one another, without prejudice against those who may come from other cultures or represent other ways of thinking. What he envisioned as a desirable or just social order we can only surmise. He lived in the context of a minor society enveloped by a vast Roman empire. The social order was local, presided over by a local satrap colluding with a religious hierarchy. The political order was embraced within a vast Roman empire that looked at local ethnic societies such as the Jews with much suspicion.

Jesus was not intimidated by this social/political order. He recognized the futility of attempting to buck the political order but focused on the inequities of the social landscape. He was particularly incensed by the privileges enjoyed by the Temple authorities (the Sadducees) and the haughtiness of the Pharisees over the poor. In contemporary terms, he was certainly not a conservative, trying to preserve the status quo or seeking a return to an illusory past glory. He obviously upset both the religious and political authorities because he was outside the mainstream and sought a better social order, much as liberals do today. Jesus was his own person. As the prophets before him, who contested royal authority, he was unique in his day.

JESUS AND THE SCOPE OF ETHICS

Jews had come to live their lives by adherence to the Law of Moses. If one adhered to the practice of the legal norms of the Law, that was sufficient. As long as one adhered to the prescriptions of the Law, taking advantage of others was acceptable. Pride and discrimination, intolerance and even persecution of the poor and defenseless – these were not a violation of the Law, according to the religious authorities of Jesus' time. These acts deeply offended Jesus and he sought to alter the social ethic in a more humane way that reflected compassion and justice.

Jesus was not content to subscribe to the common assumption that one had fulfilled his/her human commitment by simply following the written Torah, or law. He sought to impress upon people that they had a broader, more fulfilling, purpose for their lives than simply following the Law. Their purpose was to help one another, to love one another, to join together to build a reconciling community.

CHRISTIANS AND THE REAL FOLLOWERS OF JESUS

The situation Jesus encountered with the self-righteous Pharisees, the super-religious Sadducees, and the hot-headed Zealots caused him to look ahead to a better world where intolerance and injustice ceased to exist. He sought followers who would buy into this ethic and cause it to be infused into other cultures. It was not the local rulers – the Herods – or the foreign dominating authorities – the Romans - that bothered him so much as the hatreds and divisions among the common people among whom he walked from day to day.

3

HISTORIC BELIEFS

As people emerged from their primitive existence, whether in the jungle, on the plains, along rivers or elsewhere, they had already developed primitive belief systems to explain who they were, what explained the world around them and the experiences that confronted them. Over time, these beliefs became more complex and detailed, according to the society in which they lived. Stories were passed down from generation to generation as fact and became the mythology of the group, often with a consistent theme.

ORAL TRADITION

Before the advent of writing, the means for communication of information was through the oral recitation of stories, events, and technological methods and discoveries. Memorization was essential for the valid transmission of information from one generation to another. Even so, slight variations, influenced by recent events and cultural biases could creep into a narrative so that it was slightly bent from the original and modified. Many cultures transferred information from one generation to another by means of oral tradition, even into the twentieth century. American Indians continue to transmit information about their cultural history from one generation to the next in this way, as do other cultures in Africa, Australia, Asia, South America and Northern Europe.

Just as an example of how information passed by oral means can change in the retelling, gather a group of people together and begin by whispering a short narrative from the leader to the next person. Then have that person whisper the story to the next person, and so on. As the story progresses, some details will be left out while others are added. By the time the story gets to the tenth or twelfth person, it will have changed considerably.

In older societies that relied on oral transmission, the stories were usually memorized so that the accuracy of what was handed down was largely retained. Still, changes crept in over time and stories were modified according to the teller's biases, both deliberate and accidental. What is remarkable is how accurate many stories remain to the original or to verifiable historical data. That can be attributed to memorization, which is a more common feature in older, traditional societies.

But, imagine what it was like in the days before written texts were common and the means to check information against a verifiable standard was readily available. Most information was communicated orally without a means of checking its veracity. It was a climate in which truth or fact was far less important than it is today, when what you chose to believe took precedence over any desire to verify, when what you knew and believed was what your forebears taught you. With respect to what you knew or believed; it was a profoundly different world than the world we know today.

IN ANCIENT TIMES

We are jaded by the rapid and universal communications systems of the current age. But, this is only a recent development. Before the age of printing, begun in the mid-fifteenth century, the only way information could be communicated was by the spoken word or in laboriously produced handwritten form. Few people could write or read so cultures communicated orally the information they wished to transfer from generation to generation. Simple stories could be embellished as they were learned and transferred. This was not a deliberate process but merely a natural evolutionary process, with unconscious biases and newly-learned material creeping into the received story. Obviously, the storyteller wanted to impress his listeners as much as possible so it was a natural development that the story would be embellished and change over time. Since the societies were predominantly patriarchal, most of the divine characters were referred to as male.

Stories were an outcome of the questioning that people- especially young people – engaged in. "Where did I come from?" or "Where does the river start?" or "What happens to me when I die?" were all-natural queries of the young child. "What is the moon?" or "Where does the earth end?" or "Why does the sun follow the same path, day after day?" required answers.

Different cultures responded to these questions with different stories. Almost all had a Creation myth and a human origins myth. A flood story is often found and there is usually an event or place that endows the culture with unique information or rules. The natural and the supernatural are often intertwined in such a way that the culture cannot distinguish between the two. Most cultural traditions are polytheistic, but a few are monotheistic or even nontheistic (e.g. Buddhism). Spirits or supernatural forces reside in proximity and can be threatening as well as nurturing. Almost all religions have methods for placating the gods in order to achieve desired objectives – and all embrace some form of discipline and meditation. Ritual is a common element.

Hebrew culture exhibits all of these characteristics, but the traditions of belief were varied and distinct. In the early books of the Bible, we can see Priestly, Royal and Prophetic oral traditions being woven together to form a written narrative, but combined in such a way that the various biases and emphases carry through. Thus, you have two creation stories, even two Noah's Ark stories in Genesis. You have the Books of Kings and Chronicles which overlap in the telling the story of King David.

For the early Jews, the import of the story is the justification of their cultural uniqueness, amid the many different and threatening cultures surrounding them. The theology that emanates is not internally consistent. Initially, it is the Creator God who nourishes His Creation and, with His people, establishes the Covenant. Then, it is the Ruler God who demands absolute obedience to His Laws. This God dwells on the mountaintop and is sought by Moses (also reflected in many of the Psalms: "I will lift up my eyes to the hills, from whence comes my help"). There is then the Warrior God who leads His people in the invasion of the Holy Land and the fight to keep it. There is the jealous God who condemns His people from wandering off to worship other gods. There is the God of justice and righteousness, best exemplified in the oracles of the prophets, who condemns those who exploit the poor and downtrodden. And, finally, there is the Compassionate God who forgives the sins of the people and brings them back from the Exile.

At the beginning of the Christian era, there is the God of the Ark of the Covenant and of the Temple, the God who dwells in the Temple and punishes those who tread on His Holy Ground. This God requires sacrifices and offerings to placate Him from destroying the cities of Palestine. It is this God whom Jesus rejects and, as with the prophets, for whom justice and righteousness were the desired offerings.

There is little in ancient Hebrew thought about Heaven and Hell, about eternal life, and about salvation from eternal damnation. When you died, the Jews believed, your spirit went to Sheol, the abode of the dead. If there was an accounting for your sins, it was little thought of or emphasized. Your reward for piety or your punishment for wrongdoing was found in this life, not in some future Judgment Day. Read the Psalms: the righteous will be rewarded but the wicked will receive their just desserts. The Book of Job attempts to reconcile this belief with the realities of true life – but really fails to do so. Even so, there is no afterlife posited to rectify injustices. God, who is the embodiment of justice, prevails.

GNOSTICISM

There is no doubt that a Jewish Gnosticism existed before a Christian or a Judæo-Christian Gnosticism. As may be seen even in the apocalypses, since the second century B.C. gnostic thought was bound up with Judaism, which had accepted Babylonian and Syrian doctrines, dating from the time of the Exile (587-538 B.C). By the end of the first century, there were many variations of Gnostic Christianity, attempting to blend Greek Gnosticism with Christian religion. The basis of Gnosticism was "secret knowledge" leading to salvation that one obtained by being initiated into a particular group or cult. Gnostics were dualistic in their understanding of reality with the "good" opposed to the "evil" forces. Some Gnostics regarded the material world, including the human body, as evil or restraining and to be escaped, and in contrast with the realm of the spirit that was to be sought and enjoyed. For some Gnostic Christians, there were two Gods, one ruling the material earth and the other ruling the heavens. The God of the Old Testament was the source of evil and the God of the New Testament was the source of good.

Christian Gnosticism persisted into the fourth century in Asia Minor and North Africa and, at times, strongly contended with orthodox Christianity. By this time, Christianity had little to do with justice in any social or political sense and had more to do with personal salvation. In some sense, Gnosticism has always survived in some form, usually in personal devotion rather than in organized religious form.

MYSTICISM

In the early years of the 20th century, Dr. Albert Schweitzer completed his book *The Mysticism of Paul the Apostle*, an understanding of Pauline Christianity that succeeded the more common eschatological interpretation that posited the end of human history and the reign of the victorious Christ as an immanent event. Schweitzer was pointing out that, for Paul, there was a new way of living made possible with Jesus Christ, a mode of engagement for the believer so joined with Christ that the believer was now mystically unified with Him. Paul, evidencing Hellenistic influences, saw belief in Christ as leading to a new life in which the old was discarded and a new person was created. The Christian was more than simply a convert or someone who now believes in a creedal way. The believer was part of the Body of Christ with a given function to perform as though the believer would now be acting as a living Christ. For Paul, there was a spiritual union that made one a "new person in Christ".

As numbers of Christians grew and Christian communities emerged later in the first century and early in the second and spread throughout Asia Minor and the Greek Islands, Christians began to compete and contend with each other in a societal sense, while enduring a hostile political environment. The Christian character became not so much about a deep spiritual connection with the Christ but as being a member in solidarity with others who identified themselves as Christians. They saw themselves within urban communities as participants in a shared movement that gave them an identity apart from civic life. Eventually, the leaders of these Christian communities argued over doctrinal statements, wrote discourses on theology, and developed an orthodoxy that consisted of creeds to be embraced. A church hierarchy and bureaucracy developed that embraced this orthodoxy.

Nonetheless, there were others who felt the Christian connection more personally within themselves. Some adopted monastic lives and lived separately in the forest or desert, some even flagellating themselves to rid themselves of the temptations of the flesh. Others saw themselves as deeply "spiritual" within urban communities, withdrawing into private contemplation, living passively, some expressing their "spirituality" in the form of charity. They sought to identify with Christ, as Paul encouraged, in a mystical union that actually involved separation from the "things of this world". For them, a meditative life was of paramount importance.

IN THE MIDDLE AGES

Once Christianity was established as the official religion of the Roman empire under Constantine and his successors, it evolved into the more doctrinal and legalistic form that Jesus despised. But this became the characteristic of Middle Age Christianity in Europe. Religion was all about salvation from the threat of eternal damnation in a fiery Hell, epitomized in John Milton's *Paradise Lost.* The true child of God spent his/her life seeking eternal bliss through pious acts which included the veneration of the Saints and through meditation and prayer as well as (eventually) through paid Indulgences. It did not matter that you participated in the Crusades and killed many heathens. That in itself was an act that would be rewarded with salvation.

There was always a strain of Christianity that honored compassion and care for the weak. But, even though it was paid lip-service, it was certainly not a dominant strain during the Middle Ages. St. Francis and his followers, the Benedictines and some other monks in cloisters were known for their Christlike compassion. But what predominated was the adherence to the rules and creeds laid down by the early church councils and the Popes. Creative and unorthodox thought was frowned upon, even persecuted.

There were also the ascetics who chose to separate themselves from the rest of the world and, in essence, go into hiding from the trials and tribulations of the rest of the world. They were regarded as holy because of their singular devotion to the perfection of their personhood and their dedication to the achievement of heavenly salvation.

THE EARTH & EVOLUTION

A recurrence of the Medieval spirit of resistance, rejection and persecution of unorthodox thought once again broke out in the twentieth century when the issue of evolution emerged (carried over from Darwin's writings in the mid-19th century) and, in the eyes of some, threatened popular religion in the United States. Scientific explanations of the origins of the earth and of the inception of life were considered blasphemous and proponents experienced social rejection, character assassination and even loss of employment. With time, these explanations of the origins of the universe and of the formation of life on earth have survived with ever greater evidence for their veracity.

The problem has been that the Biblical story of Creation has been taken as a scientific explanation of Creation and not as an allegorical narrative written by a pre-scientific people who were trying to explain where they came from, to whom they owed their lives, the reason for their existence and their mutual obligations for life and behavior. It's always easier to embrace a traditional story than to adhere to a novel explanation that goes against the culturally accepted folklore.

We live in a modern time, when the information gleaned by science has provided for us wonders never dreamed of only a few years ago, from refrigerators to MRI equipment at the hospital, from knowledge of the galaxies to insights into the construction of the atom, from chemicals to transform and save life to procedures to transplant internal organs. We no longer believe much of the mythologies of the recent past.

And so, it is with the understanding of where we came from. Life has evolved over the vast expanse of time and humans have evolved from earlier forms of life to what we are today. We are the result of a natural process we now call evolution. There is nothing sacrilegious or heretical about that. The problem is that we once thought that belief in God was dependent upon the Creation of the physical world. That is not what it was about. For Jesus, what the world and human life in it were about was how we behaved in the world.

RELIGION

There are many religions in the world. Christianity is only one of them. Try to hold one up against the other and it will be hard to decide among them which is the most authentic and moral. In the name of the god of whatever religion, atrocities were committed, even in benign Buddhism. There is always a way to justify the killing of someone else, whether of the same religion or of some different religion. On the other hand, most if not all religions contribute to social good, at least at one time or another.

So, what is religion, and how does it differ from other ethical beliefs or ritual practices or even political and social views and commitments? Is it belief in a Higher Authority? Or, the practice of a regular ritual? Is it belief in a soul and an afterlife? Is it a commitment to a certain doctrine of morality? Or, a statement of faith, premised upon an assertion of beliefs which cannot be proven? The dictionary defines "religion" as "Belief in and reverence for a supernatural power recognized as the creator and governor of the universe" or "A particular integrated system of this expression" or "an objective pursued with zeal or conscientious devotion".

When the Founding Fathers of the United States wrote that there could be no establishment of religion in this country, they had in mind the religious squabbles between denominations and between Catholics and Protestants that had torn Europe apart in the Medieval era and had left millions prematurely dead. They had no concept of Zoroastrianism, Buddhism, Hinduism, Islam, Agnosticism or Atheism and, even here in the U.S., in years to follow, persecutions and ostracisms were carried on. There are groups, such as the Masons, Lions, Rotary, Common Cause and Libertarians that have certain common beliefs that hold them together. Yet, they are not considered to be religions. What makes the difference? Buddhists and Unitarians do not necessarily espouse belief in God or gods or supernatural powers, yet they are classified as religions and are recognized as such by the U.S. Government. The Unitarian-Universalists and the Scientologists are such groups.

I doubt that we will ever find a definition upon which we can agree. So, we will have to create a definition that we can use for practical purposes. We could start by accepting self- designations, groups that register with the government as organized religions. Of course, there are some religions that do not take an organized form but clearly exhibit the characteristics of a religion.

4

THE SOCIAL & POLITICAL CONTEXT

The Political & Social Context of Old Testament Judaism

Apart from the Biblical account, the evidence for the Hebrew people leaving Egypt around 1200 BCE is scanty. There is no independent historical record for the Hebrew people before that time and the Biblical account of events prior to the Egyptian residence must be attributed to folklore and oral transmission. Even the Egyptian residence and the events recounted of the Exodus, the forty years in the desert, the invasion of Palestine and the years of the judges must be regarded skeptically. Not until the ascension of David and the establishment of Jerusalem as the capital of the United Kingdom in 1000 BCE can we be confident that the Biblical history is anything more than folklore.

The Biblical Context: Hebrew Origins

The Book of Exodus is not merely a historical account of the Jewish departure from Egypt, it contains the rules – or law – for faithful obedience to Yahweh and for communal living, including the Ten Commandments (Exodus 20). There is additional Law ("and God said to Moses") contained in Leviticus and Numbers – and a summary of the Law given in Deuteronomy (the second Law) which was apparently composed later during the Babylonian Captivity (587-543 BCE).

But the Law stated in Exodus through Numbers likely originated and accreted, at least in part, in the pre-Davidic period before 1000 BCE and represents the glue that drew the twelve ancient Hebrew tribes together. Its code dealt primarily with conduct among the people (altercations, sexual conduct, business activities) as well as among the tribes but not with social justice issues. This tribal and social unity lasted through the reigns of David and his son Solomon but broke apart in 963 BCE with Solomon's death and the royal ascension of Jeroboam in the south (Judah) and Rehoboam in the north (Israel).

In 721 B.C.E., Israel fell to Assyrian forces and the captives were led off to exile in Nineveh. Syria then fell in 609 to Babylonia that then, in 587, conquered Judah and carried its leadership off to exile in Babylon, the Exile lasting until 538 B.C.E. when the Jewish people were allowed to return. The Exile in Babylon was especially critical for the Jewish people for it created a self-aware identity that survives to this day. It was also a time of great priestly activity in the formulation of ritual that also survives in the modern Jewish community. Much of the Biblical literature (including the Book of Deuteronomy) was composed during this time of Exile.

GREEK & ROMAN OCCUPIERS OF PALESTINE

In 336, pursuant to the conquests of Alexander the Great, Palestine came under Greek dominance, eventually throwing it off under the Maccabees, but succumbing to Roman rule in 63 BCE. Hellenistic and then Roman influences crept into Judean life despite attempts at resistance. Under Roman rule, the Herods derived from the Maccabees and became the local surrogate despots. In first century Judea, the Jews came to despise both the Herods and the Romans, with the Zealots leading the opposition. It was in this context that Jesus came of age and gathered followers for his teaching. Suspicious of any nonconformity, the Herods and Roman authorities conspired to get rid of this rabble-rouser.

THE BIBLICAL CONTEXT OF THE FIRST CENTURY

Pursuant to the Crucifixion of Jesus, his followers appeared to coalesce around his disciples and his family, his teachings, his memory. They were vehemently opposed by the local Jewish leaders and priests, even to the point of stoning at least one of the followers (Stephen). According to the Book of Acts, written by a follower (Luke) in the latter part of the first century, the earliest Christians in Jerusalem attempted to live communally, pooling all that they owned (Acts 4), an experiment that apparently did not succeed for it is not mentioned again.

A Pharisee who observed the stoning of Stephen, Saul of Tarsus, emerged to embrace this Jewish "Heresy" and eventually, as Paul the apostle, began to spread the Gospel on various trips throughout the Hellenistic world, periodically being rejected and imprisoned. With Christian congregations developing in several communities throughout Asia Minor and westward into Europe, Roman authorities began to notice and to take oppressive action. Until the fourth century, when Constantine embraced Christianity, Christians were living in a hostile world, suffering various intensities of persecution, ordered by the Roman emperors. It appears that their primary concerns were for the welfare of one another in a hostile environment and only rarely for their pagan brethren. Issues of social justice (slavery, civil rights, discrimination, social poverty, etc.) were not primary concerns in the early Christian community.

THE CHURCH IN ITS EARLY YEARS

For the first two hundred and fifty years following the Crucifixion, despite living a precarious existence evidenced by Roman persecution, the Christian community expanded and flourished throughout the empire, winning converts from people at all echelons of the social strata. Christians met secretly in the homes of its adherents for worship, celebration of Baptism and the Eucharist and discussion among themselves. United against the cruelty and tyranny of the Roman authorities, these conditions contributed to a social camaraderie and a shared knowledge and belief as well as a mutual concern for the well-being of one another. The leaders of these communities became known as elders and bishops. The more learned and thoughtful among them composed memoranda about Christian beliefs which they shared with others, developing an orthodox theology in the process.

During this period, as Prof. Bart Ehrman has shown (in *Lost Scriptures*), there were many variations of Christian belief. In a situation where mobility was limited, Christian groups tended to become ingrown about the Gospel accounts and apostolic letters they used and developed particular variations of the nature of Christ. There were Montanists (who tended to venerate the laws of the Old Testament, the Gnostics (who regarded the special knowledge Christ imparted as essential for salvation), Donatists (in North Africa, who believed that one must lead a faultless life to have access to the Sacraments) and adherents of Mysticism (who sought an otherworldly unity with the deity), among many others. However, bishops (local church leaders) appear to have visited one another in small groups to discuss theology and gradually formed an orthodox belief that excluded other more aberrant beliefs. These early gatherings were fairly local but gradually the need for a unified hierarchy and orthodoxy developed, culminating in the Council of Nicaea in 322 A.D. The focus on the nature of God and Christ took preeminence and the ethic of Jesus toward others was relegated to the background.

In 313 A, D., Emperor Constantine declared the Christian community legitimate and, except for a brief period following, the church became an authorized presence in the empire. No longer being persecuted, the church rapidly grew in numbers at the expense of the pagan rituals of Rome. The dynamic changed from one of a secret and self-protective community to one of social prevalence and widespread acceptance. It was no longer dangerous to be a Christian and morphed into a preferred social identity.

THE CHURCH IN THE MIDDLE AGES (FROM THE SIXTH CENTURY UNTIL THE SIXTEENTH CENTURY)

With no further interference from the political authorities, the church became more institutional in its structure, less communal and more imbued with mystical characteristics. The sense of closeness and interdependency was displaced with ritual and religious obligation. The church itself became more integrated with secular authority, with the result that the political authorities became more active in enforcing religious orthodoxy and practice, thereby enhancing their own authority. In this context, monasticism arose, often distained by church authorities because it could not be controlled. This alignment of church and political authority depressed any movement for political or ecclesiastical reform and corruption crept into these institutions. All sense of what Jesus sought to achieve was lost and he became solely an instrument for salvation in the hereafter. Christian ethics was narrowly aligned with anything allowed by the church.

The Sacraments of Baptism, Confirmation and the Eucharist became rites of passage for any legitimate Christian citizen. Thus, one was baptized as an infant into the local community as a matter of incipient citizenship. As one grew older, after a ceremony of Confirmation, one was admitted to the mystical society of the blessed and permitted to receive the Eucharist, with the belief that the elements were believed to be the actual body and blood of Christ, the doctrine of Transubstantiation. To be a Christian meant that one was a participant in a group of those who paid a nominal confession of belief. Once included in the group, it was implicit that one would accept the other supernatural beliefs of Immaculate Conception of Mary, Mariolatry, the belief that Mary could intercede for one's for salvation, the Assumption of Mary. Expanding on this was the belief in the intercession of Saints, the holiness of the Bible, the magical powers of sacred objects, including Icons and things such as the St. Christopher's medal and statuettes. Christianity's focus became the salvation of one's soul rather than the cause of justice and righteousness in communal society.

For a thousand years, being a Christian was the accepted norm, at least in Europe. Church buildings and institutions became the center of community life. Priests became powerful politically and church rituals, both personal and communal, became pervasive in life. Conformity with the dominant social institutions became identified with acting as a Christian and was the accepted norm, the right and proper way to live. There was nothing unique about being a Christian. In fact, to question anything in the social order or contrary to the church's teaching was to transgress being a Christian.

In such an environment where it was blasphemous to depart from orthodox church doctrine and where the search for truth became anathema, the liberation that Jesus talked about ("the truth shall set you free") was totally reversed and was subject to punishment. However, the ability of the church to tolerate uncounted expressions of church life was remarkable. There was not only the village parish, there were huge urban parishes and unique isolationist communities. You could be a lone ascetic or the member of a brotherly or sisterly order – and there were many of them, founded by various leaders for a variety of purposes. Some communities existed for orphan care, some for health care, some to aid impoverished & homeless folk, some as militants to defend the church against hostile forces.

THE INSTITUTION

The church became the dominant feature in life – and enforced conformity. As the central organizing institution, it grew wealthy, building huge cathedrals in urban settings, sponsoring marvelous works of art and music, engaging in such business pursuits as wine making, and sponsoring public festivals and events. The Bible was no longer accessible to the common folk and became the exclusive property of the clergy. Ritual rather than personal expression became the dominant form of religious life, reducing spontaneity to a dangerous corner of life.

Bishoprics developed early in the church as leaders took on the role of coordinating activities and beliefs among churches. Well before the time of Constantine, bishops were gathering to discuss doctrine and organization – and defenses against hostile authorities. But, once Christianity became the accepted state religion of the Roman Empire, bishops gained substantial political strength, resulting in corruption and the deterioration of its beneficence toward the people.

THE SACRAMENTS

Baptism was simply a waypoint in life, signifying that one was now a part of the general community, the charge for Christian growth diminishing in importance. It was now a rite of passage for one to become an adult. The sense of responsibility on how to lead one's life was diminished.

The mystery of the Eucharist now became the central and most important feature of the religious life. It didn't matter how one lived his/her life so long as he/she participated in the celebration of the Eucharist as frequently as possible. Living a compassionate life as a follower of Jesus receded in importance. The Mass became even more central and the mystery of life became more profound when the church declared that, in the Eucharist, the actual wine and wafer were actually transformed in the actual Body and Blood of Jesus Christ: the Doctrine of Transubstantiation.

Baptism and the Eucharist were the two primary Sacraments. In time, other practices were accorded the status of Sacraments: Confirmation, Penance (Confession), Holy Orders, Matrimony, Extreme Unction (Last Rites). Church beliefs were also expanded during the Middle Ages, more by popular circulation than by theological decree from above.

OTHER PRACTICES AND SACRAMENTS
OF THE ROMAN CATHOLIC CHURCH

Over the course of the Middle Ages, the Roman Catholic Church developed a list of ritualistic practices that it added to what it considered Sacraments. It was formalized as late as 1439 although the church attributes each as being instituted by Jesus. **Baptism** and the **Eucharist (Last Supper or communion)** were obviously the original Sacraments that were practiced by followers from the very beginning, being handed down from Jesus. While it claims that the remaining five were instituted by Jesus during the time of his ministry, they were elevated to the level of Sacrament at various times following the Church's recognition by Constantine and his successors. **Penance** for the forgiveness of sins (aka repentance) was obviously one of the first practices to be recognized by the end of the second century as it was a foundation principle of the religious life for followers of Jesus. It is likely that **Holy Orders** was recognized formally as a church feature early in the second century since church leaders were acknowledged as deacons and priests. Regional leaders were called bishops shortly thereafter. Still, ordination to these three classes of Holy Orders was likely not formalized until a short time later. **Marriage** was a civil function that was absorbed by the church early in the third century but not accorded Sacramental status until much later. **Confirmation** meant formally identifying one as a member or adherent to the church was also probably fairly early in practice although not elevated to the status of a Sacrament until the fifth or sixth century. **Extreme Unction (Last rites)** developed as a blessing for the dying but was not regarded with Sacramental status until the 12th or 13th century.

These practices are generally performed in some way by the Protestant churches today but are not accorded the same honor as Baptism and the Lord's Supper. Note that each of these Sacraments or practices has to do with one's individual status and has nothing to do with one's responsibility as a humanitarian (fulfilling Jesus' command to "Go into all the world") or as a responsible participant in the larger community (the world). It has to do with one's "religious" life, and, with the possible exception of marriage, not with one's communal relationships. Following the lead of the Apostle Paul, the church was drifting further away from the communal responsibility emphasized by Jesus.

CHURCH PRACTICES AND BELIEFS

The Veneration of Mary

The veneration of Mary goes back to the end of the first century when she was ascribed a role in the process of salvation by one of the early martyrs. Gradually, Mary was understood as having an important role in Christian life and the first church dedicated to Mary was Santa Maria Maggiore, built in Rome between 430 & 440 A.D. In 431, Mary was declared the "Mother of God" by the Council of Ephesus and her importance has been gradually enhanced ever since. Her role has been assigned as a caregiver and a healer, but she has never been assigned a more activist role as a reformer of social mores.

Immaculate Conception: Mariolatry & the Assumption

Because Mary was said to be the mother of Jesus, she had to be without sin. Thus, the doctrine of the Immaculate Conception was declared, wherein Mary was determined to have been naturally conceived by her mother Anne, but without sin, remaining so throughout her life. Again, what should have been regarded as a natural life was determined during the Middle Ages to have involved the intervention of God to eliminate sin from her character.

Sacred Features

The long period of the Middle Ages allowed an extensive period for the trappings of the church to take form since it was going through a time of religious emphasis with social activism largely neglected. The attempt to make society more compassionate and respectful of human rights was cast aside in favor of a more personally intimate mode of living.

The Bible

As we have seen, the New Testament writings date from the period 60 A.D. through the end of the first century. These Gospel narratives and epistles were read aloud in the early churches by literate leaders since many of the early Christians were unable to read. Thus, the Biblical writings became the property of the clergy and were unavailable by default to the laymen. The Councils of Hippo (325 A.D.), and Carthage (397 A.D.) define twenty seven documents as authentic and legitimate for inclusion as sacred Scripture, But, popular access was discouraged as well as translation into languages other than Latin, a practice that intensified throughout the Middle Ages. In 1415, the Council of Constance condemned John Wycliffe for his translation of the Bible into English in 1384. Although he survived, William Tyndale was executed for the same crime in 1536.

Both men were rebels against the more exclusivist roles and doctrines of the Roman Catholic Church in the 15th and 16th centuries – and sought to make religious study and activity more accessible to the common person. However, with Martin Luther's Ninety-five Theses made public in Wittenberg, Germany in 1517 and his subsequent translation of the Bible into German so that it could be available to everyone, the inhibition against Bible reading by the laity was ended. This was a highly significant development since it meant that the authoritarian control of the church over all intellectual activity was coming to an end. Not only were religion and theology affected but also philosophy, scientific studies and mathematics were no longer the province of a single controlling entity but were democratized. The right of a person to pursue his/her chosen intellectual studies was now liberated, leading to the more participatory governments we know today.

Magical Objects

The Middle Ages gave rise to a multiplicity of Icons such as the Rosary and St. Christopher's Medal. A Rosary is a set of prayer beads that is intended to win the intercession of Mary for the relief of a burden or the winning of a holy objective by the person making use of the beads. The Rosary is based on the long-standing custom established by <u>Pope Pius V</u> in the 16th century, grouping the mysteries in three sets: the Joyful Mysteries, the Sorrowful Mysteries, and the Glorious Mysteries. The Christopher Medal is based on the life of Christopher, a <u>martyr</u> killed in the reign of the 3rd-century Roman Emperor <u>Decius</u> (reigned 249–251) or alternatively under the Roman Emperor <u>Maximinus II Daia</u> (reigned 308–313) who, according to legend, carried a child, who was unknown to him, across a river before the child revealed himself as Christ. Therefore, he is the <u>patron saint</u> of travelers, and small images of him are often worn around the neck, on a bracelet, carried in a pocket, or placed in vehicles by those who believe in its efficacy. His veneration only appears late in Christian tradition, and did not become widespread in the Western Church until the <u>Late Middle Ages</u>, although churches and monasteries were named after him by the 7th century.

Prayers to Change Things

It is common to people of all cultures that they have sought to change misfortunes, current or potential, by means of some form of supplication to the gods or entities who have control of things. In the Western world that is characterized by Christianity, this has taken the form of prayer. Among other iconic objects, the Rosary and the Christopher Medal are exemplary of such things. Even today, among pagans or non-believers, people seem to resort to prayer in times of distress or danger. This was certainly true of the Middle Ages when medicine and rescue equipment and communication devices were primitive or non-existent. Prayer was the only recourse one had to obtain relief.

Canonization

As today, there are heroes who provide sustenance, escape from danger or comfort. A few stand out. The way to recognize such people was to Canonize them and declare them as saints, albeit posthumously. The practice continues in the Roman and Orthodox churches to this day, although it dates back to the early church and the Middle Ages. There were those who perished as martyrs rather than succumb to the whims of the political and ecclesiastical authorities. Some were truly saintly; others were rascals who, nonetheless, subsequent generations came to revere and declared as saints, though undeservedly so.

THE CHURCH SINCE THE REFORMATION:

With Martin Luther's post of the 95 Theses on the door of the Wittenberg church in 1517, the landscape was opened widely to a proliferation of breakaway churches from Rome. With the Calvinists in Geneva, the Reformed churches in Germany and the Low Countries, the Anabaptists throughout the continent, the Calvinists again in Scotland and the Church of England throughout the British kingdom, religious as well as political disunity throughout Europe abounded and gave an impetus to the Roman Church's Inquisition which was already underway, but broadened to include political dissidents. Religion was politicized but its social and humanitarian proclivities were crushed.

THE CHURCH SINCE 1600
(THE PAST FIVE CENTURIES)

The Industrial Revolution in the 18th century sparked a renewed interest in the plight of the poor in society, initially in England (as evidenced in the works of Charles Dickens) and then spreading to the Continent. However, the state church system in many places inhibited social reform since the church represented the government and the head of state held sway in both places. Late in the 19th century, the labor movement and the suffrage movement gained momentum and, while it took time for these forces to strengthen into potent political forces, their goals were largely achieved in the early 20th century. Churches were heavily involved in providing support and encouragement. Child labor, mental health issues, prison reform and health care advanced during this same period.

It was the issue of Evolution that the church saw as its major challenge in the early 20th century. Although Charles Darwin published the Origin of the Species in 1858, the discussion over the Theory of Evolution was primarily academic in Europe in the late 19th century and only became a huge religious controversy in the early 20th century. More liberal clergy saw Evolution as a process by which God created life forms, but conservative clergy saw it as a direct confrontation of the literal Biblical story and denounced it throughout the century. Interestingly, the controversy around Evolution occurred at almost the same time as the Social Gospel made its appearance. Walter Rauschenbush and other clergy interpreted the Christian Gospel through the eyes of social reformers and sought to influence the church as the instrument for social change within society.

THE CHURCH TODAY

With the end of the Depression and the close of the Second World War in 1945, there was a great resurgence of church involvement, largely in the various denominations in the United States. Churches flourished and had well-financed budgets financing recovery efforts in Europe and agricultural and health missions elsewhere. At the same time, more conservative, independent churches were beginning to appear on the scene with considerable success at drawing denominational refugees over to their congregations. As denominational involvement has decreased over the past half century, independent "Bible" churches have increased substantially, favoring a literal interpretation of Scriptures, eschewing scientific findings, embracing the anti-abortion movement, and supporting politically conservative policies and candidates. In their missionary efforts, they have extended their activities overseas and provide health, agricultural and other services in order to win converts. For the most part, they take no political positions and do their best to accommodate to authoritarian regimes.

Denominational churches have seen their church numbers decline and their congregations shrink and age. Budgets, too, have been steadily cut over the past three or four decades so that their support of community activities has also diminished. Nonetheless, churches have sought to replace financial support with other kinds of activities such as providing refugee and homeless shelters, food banks, clothing depots, etc.

THE BIBLE

BIBLIOLATRY

On the cover, it reads "HOLY BIBLE". People display it – but rarely read it. People revere it, pay it homage, but tend to dismiss it. They carry it in their breast pocket, hoping it will absorb a stray bullet. They use it as a magical icon, hoping it will bring them good luck. But few know its content. They pay it lip service – as the greatest book ever written but put it aside to read steamy detective novels – or watch inane TV programs.

Those who read the Bible carefully, understand that it contains writing that is not so holy, that it represents many different points of view, that it was written at various times and under varying but specific conditions – that are not particularly pertinent to today's world. It is a fallible document, written by people, most of whom were understanding their world as inhabited by God, to whom they owed their faith and allegiance.

To hold the Bible up as a sacred icon is sacrilege and to fail to understand it. To do so is called Bibliolatry, the worship of a divine fetish with magical powers that can be manipulated to increase the odds of achieving one's objectives and good fortune. Bibliolatry has no place in a Christian faith or in a modern world.

AS CHRISTIAN SOURCEBOOK

The Canon

The Books of the Bible, 39 in the Old Testament and 27 in the New Testament (as provided in the Bible used by Protestants), were determined by an inexact process over a lengthy period of time. What is called the Old Testament by Christians was presumably determined by the Rabbinic Council of Jamnia at the end of the first century of the Christian era, following a lengthy time of traditional use by the Jewish community. Christians accepted the books of the canon which were translated into Latin in the Vulgate in the fourth century. The books that comprise the Old Testament canon differ between Christian Churches as well as their order and names. The most common Protestant canon comprises 39 books, the Catholic canon comprises 46 books (including the books of the Maccabean saga), and the canons of the Eastern Orthodox and Oriental Orthodox Churches comprise up to 51 books.[ ]. The 39 books in common to all the Protestant Christian canons corresponds to 24 books of the Jewish *Tanakh*, with some differences of order, plus some differences in text.

The books included in the New Testament were finally determined in the third century of the Christian era after a considerable period of dispute. As Bart Ehrman discloses in *Lost Scriptures*, there were other Gospels (narratives of the life of Jesus) as well as other epistle-type documents floating around in the second century and representing various interpretations of who Jesus was. Gradually, with arguments over the proper interpretation of the nature of Jesus, an orthodox canon was agreed upon. Disputes continued over inclusion of The Shepherd of Hermas, the Revelation of John, and other writings.

Biblical Forms of Literature

The Books of the Old and New Testaments are Divided into Several Types or Categories. In the Old Testament, primarily contained in the early books of Genesis through Judges, there is a considerable amount of orally transmitted Folklore that was eventually written down. Then, there are the Historical books that are presumably fairly accurate records of the Hebrew/Jewish people from the time of David (1000 B.C.) until the rebuilding of the Temple under Nehemiah around 515 B.C. There are the Prophetic books from Isaiah & Jeremiah through the time of Habakkuk. There is Poetry (Psalms, Ecclesiastes< etc.) and other Literature (Proverbs). And, finally, there is the Apocalyptic writing of the Book of Daniel. Esther, which fails to mention God but calls the Jewish people to be firm in resistance to foreign influences, might fall into this category as well. The legal prescriptions and the genealogies are generally woven into the Torah (first five books) but probably date from the period of the Exile in the sixth century B.C.)

The Several Categories of New Testament Writings

In the New Testament, there are the Gospels, the historical book of Acts, the Epistles and the Apocalypse of Revelation. Each of these various forms was considered important enough to be included in the Canon. But, it would be well to understand that the purpose of each was somewhat different from the others. When reading the Bible, know what you are reading. The stories from Genesis are simply a means of transmitting a cultural identity and an explanation of things that are. The prophets need to be understood in the context of their own time and are not necessarily relevant to the current situation. The poetry is beautiful writing, often sung. The history records events that the people can look back to in order to understand who they are and why they are in their current situation.

The Truth of the Bible

Removing Bible verses from the context in which they were written is to misinterpret a true understanding of the literature. Everything was written in a historical setting and influenced by what was going on at the time. To think that Biblical statements invariably apply to the present time is simply misleading, especially where Apocalypse, Parousia or End of Time prescriptions are concerned. Every age has had "prophets" who have said the end of time is at hand. All have been wrong. On the other hand, the Biblical writers have been consistent in encouraging righteousness and justice and respectfulness toward humankind and God.

Comment: The Bible as the Word of God

In the early years of Christianity, there were various writings that went around among the churches, letters from Paul and others offering counsel and advice as well as theological ideas. These writings were gradually sorted out and the New Testament was formed with the Old Testament canon transmitted from the Jewish authorities. The Canon, as noted, was not assembled until the fourth century. Yet, even then, it was only a source of instruction and inspiration, not an absolutely definitive and exclusive source of the faith.

The Bible, of course, was written in Hebrew, Aramaic and Greek but was translated into the Latin Vulgate, the version used for years by the church in Rome. The Orthodox church, based in Constantinople, used Greek texts for the New Testament and the Septuagint (a Greek translation of the Hebrew Bible) for the Old Testament.

Throughout the Middle Ages, the Bible became the exclusive property of the church. While portions of it were read to laymen in services of worship, it became physically unavailable to them. Only when Luther and his fellow reformers translated it into the vernacular did it become the property of the people. The printing press made it more accessible, but, in the process, it began to take on the aura of a fetish, a holy icon with special properties of its own.

In our time, the King James Version became, in the eyes of some, the only God-inspired version of the Bible and other versions were condemned as perversions. Modern scholarship, more authentic Hebrew and Greek texts, and the desire for less archaic language eventually forced critics to accept new translations.

The Bible has only temporarily been regarded as a static document. Throughout the years, with new findings of ancient manuscripts, with newer scholarship into the meanings of words, and with the revelations of other documents, the text has been modified. There never was, and never will be, a final version of the Bible, one that is unerringly the Word of God.

The Truth of the Bible: Evangelicals start with the premise that the Bible is the "Word of God" rather than a discovery of whatever truth it contains. Billy Graham used to say: "The Bible says…." as though the Bible should be given unquestioning authoritative acceptance and that it is a uniform vessel of truth, undifferentiated in its content and sourced from the same Author. It is inductive reasoning to assume that the Bible has a single point of view, that it contains a uniform message and that it is divinely authored or even inspired by a controlling force. Inductive reasoning is false logic and begins with a premise that is unsubstantiated.

THE NATIVITY FABLE

Everyone loves the Nativity story at Christmastime. In most churches, it is regarded as a historical event. But, it is hardly that. What it is is a narrative that developed among followers of Jesus of Nazareth to explain his birth and appearance. The Nativity story we know is actually a conflation of two different stories written by Matthew and Luke. The common elements are few. The differences, though they do not necessarily conflict, are substantial.

The first Gospel written (of the four Gospels in the Bible) is Mark, probably written around 60 A.D., almost thirty years after the crucifixion of Jesus. Mark appears to know nothing about the birth of Jesus. There is no genealogy given in Mark. His Gospel begins with John the Baptist at the Jordan River – and progresses on to tell about Jesus coming to John to be baptized. How did Mark's Gospel come to be? Probably as a result of oral transmission of the story of Jesus over many years, perhaps even to consolidate some conflicting earlier narratives, thus requiring a written account that could be referred to as authoritative.

About ten years later, probably around 70 to 80 A.D., the Gospels of Matthew and Luke were written. Both Gospels give a genealogy for Jesus, through David, the glorious King who ruled over Israel and Judah, the united Kingdom, about a thousand years earlier. Oddly, though, these genealogies are only partly the same. The first third is the same, the rest is not – until the fathers immediately prior to Joseph. But, what is also odd is that Joseph is supposedly NOT the father of Jesus, since, according to both Matthew and Luke, Jesus was conceived by the Holy Spirit. So, why is the genealogy carried up to Joseph? Note, incidentally, that Matthew says the father of Joseph is Heli whereas Luke says that the father of Joseph is Jacob. Their intent is undoubtedly to give Jesus a genealogical link to King David. Note, however, that the word that is used for virgin can also be defined as "young woman", leaving the possibility that Jesus was conceived in the normal way. It is possible that Matthew, at least, did not posit the virgin birth but that the verses (2:19-20) that recount the virgin birth were added at a later time.

Nonetheless, both Matthew and Luke posit that Mary will conceive the child, although being a virgin. in response to the message of her conception of a child, she exclaims "How can this be, since I have no husband?" In Luke, it is stated, that Jesus was conceived "before they came together". The idea that Jesus was born of a virgin is replicated in other situations in ancient times in order to support the idea of divine intervention. In this case, the idea was probably circulated among the early Christians and then incorporated by the Gospel writers in order to give credence and support to the idea that Jesus was conceived by the Holy Spirit. Early Christians, believing that Jesus was of divine origin, could have, in the oral tradition that Luke coopted, have built the narrative of the Virgin Birth in order to justify their belief that Jesus was more than a mere human being.

Note also another peculiarity. Mary's conversation with the Holy Spirit (Lk. 1:34-35) is a private conversation. Then, later, according to Luke, Mary goes to the home of Elizabeth in Judea. There she utters the poetic statement we know as the Magnificat, only in the presence of Elizabeth. Who was present to hear and write down these exclamations? How were they recorded? We don't know. It's a curiosity how they made it into Luke's Gospel. The suggestion is that they were actually composed in oral transmission or possibly by Luke himself to fill out his story and make it a religious tribute to Mary. It is interesting that, although Mary and Joseph are "betrothed", there is no subsequent mention of a marriage ceremony. When Matthew says they fled to Egypt, were they married by then or still only "betrothed"?

Both Matthew & Luke write about the birth of Jesus – but their stories are different. Matthew wrote about the Wise Men from the East, coming to find Jesus by following the star. Herod instructs them to bring him news of where Jesus can be found, but the Wise Men, after finding him, depart by another way so that they do not need to report back to Herod. Nonetheless, Herod proceeds to murder all the Jewish boys of two years of age or less. To escape this slaughter, Mary and Joseph flee to Egypt. When they return, after Herod has died, they go to Nazareth, as though that is a new locale for them. That's the Nativity story for Matthew. Incidentally, although Herod was widely hated for his cruelties and was guilty of killing members of his family and many military officers during the last three years of his reign, most historians doubt the Slaughter of the Innocents story since it is recorded nowhere else than in Matthew. It is likely that the story is folklore.

The common element of Matthew with Luke is that Jesus is born in Bethlehem. In Luke, Mary & Joseph are from Nazareth and go to Jerusalem for the census whereas, as noted above, the origin of Mary & Joseph is unknown to Matthew, but Nazareth is adopted as their home after they return from Egypt. In Luke, we have the story of the shepherds out in the fields, keeping watch over their sheep by night. Mark & Matthew know nothing of this story – nor does John, the latest Gospel, written around 90 – 100 A.D. This suggests that the Nativity stories in Matthew & Luke were developed in different Christian communities and each story was not known to the other. Writing even later, John either did not know these Nativity stories or else did not believe they were important or true.

The only common elements of the Nativity stories written by Matthew and Luke are as follows:

- Jesus is born in Bethlehem;
- Jesus' is born of Mary, who is a virgin at the time of conception. Mary is betrothed to Joseph;
- Following Jesus' birth, the family goes to Nazareth to live.

The "kinswoman" relationship of Mary and Elizabeth ((Lk.1:36), the Manger story, the Wise Men, the Shepherds, the Slaughter of the Innocents, the Flight to Egypt- none of these elements of the Nativity story are common to more than one of the Gospel writers and are unknown to the other three. The obvious conclusion is that the Nativity stories were developed independently in separate Christian communities in the forty years following the crucifixion; then written down separately. John's Gospel, written even later than the Synoptic Gospels, ignores the Nativity stories but gives a theological prologue that posits the existence of the Son with the Father from the beginning of time. The first common element of all four Gospels begins with the appearance of John the Baptist and the Baptism of Jesus in the river Jordan.

The Christmas story is a time-honored, beautiful story that is worthy of being remembered and retold. But it is not to be regarded as literal fact. It is poetic folklore and is to be regarded as a testimony to the unique presence of Jesus among his followers, the attempt of ancient Christians to regard the Master they followed and for whom they were persecuted and sometimes died as a gift from the Father. For that, we honor them – and remember Jesus as an exemplary figure to follow.

Is the Bible true in all its history and in all its prescriptive sayings? Is the Law it dictates in Leviticus and elsewhere

THE HISTORY OF THE OLD & NEW TESTAMENTS

Are the laws given in the Old Testament eternally and universally inviolate? Are the quotations found in various parts of the Bible compatible with one another? Let's look at the Bible and understand how it was composed and assembled, who wrote the books of the Bible and why, and when the books were written and what were the circumstances of its composition. Then we can decide how Holy it is and to what extent it could be a source of guidance and inspiration for our lives.

In Ecclesiastes, for example, the writer says "Vanity of vanities, all is vanity" something that hardly squares with the purposeful attitude of Paul and his contemporary evangelists. Let's see what the Jewish experience was before the advent of the Christian era and consider how the Old Testament came to be. Let's look at Jesus and see the man who really walked the roads of Palestine before the legends crept in. We will view the early Christian era to consider the distortions that took place. And, let's look at worship practices today and see how meaningful they are. And, let's look at what a meaningful Christian life could be in the modern world.

It is hard, then, to claim that the Bible is true in every respect. In fact, Biblical contradictions, competing accounts of events and different perspectives and philosophies (viz, Job, Psalms, and Micah) reveal it as more of a compendium of different viewpoints than as a monolithic statement of divine thought.

ORAL TRADITION AND TRANSMISSION

Have you ever formed a circle with a few people and whispered a story from person to person? The first person starts with a printed story that he/she reads, then whispers it to the person next to him/her. Around the circle it goes, then the last person to hear the story tells it to the entire group. Is it the same story that was started around the circle? What details dropped out? What was added? How much different than the original is the final telling of the story?

Imagine how a story changes over time: a month, a year, a decade, several decades. Perhaps a story remains fairly consistent with its original purpose – but the details have changed. It's almost certain to happen. It probably will be influenced by the change in peripherally-related events over a period of time.

If the sayings and stories were transmitted orally over a lengthy period of time before being written down, it is likely they were selected, interpreted, changed and rearranged by the scribe and influenced by his/her own experiences and biases. But, let's be as generous as we can be for the integrity of the material.

We don't know when the sayings of Jesus - or the events in his life – were first written down. Perhaps soon after they were spoken or took place. Undoubtedly, they were again selected to conform to the author's own experience and biases. They were interpreted according to who the author was. Once written, they had a degree of permanency, but if a subsequent author used the earlier material in composing a more complete narrative, that author also selected and arranged the original material. That process is evidenced by the way in which Matthew and Luke recorded the sayings of Jesus in what we know as the Sermon on the Mount in Matthew and the Sermon on the Plain in Luke.

Give the Biblical books a break rather than making assumptions about what they are and where they came from. Consider them newfound writings which you are going to explore, just as you would any ancient documents. Consider what the material says and evaluate its contents in an objective manner, without preconceptions. It is literature from an earlier age, positing a pre-scientific worldview and reflecting the thoughts and preconceptions of an earlier time, reflecting various political and social biases of the authors. Some were mere poets, others were defenders of the monarchy, others were priests and religious authorities, some were early historians and others were simply storytellers. They did not all come from the same time and, thus, reflected the political and social situations of their day. Some were critics of the socio-political environment in which they found themselves, others were more complacent. They came with different concerns and viewpoints: contrast the pessimism of the author of Job with the Psalmists' assurance that the righteous will be rewarded (Psalm 23). Obviously, the writers of the Biblical material were educated and literate, in contrast to the vast majority of people who were uneducated and non-literate. But, they did not all agree, and arguments can be found within the books of the Bible, in both Old and New Testaments. You just need to look.

THE HISTORY OF THE OLD TESTAMENT

The Pre-Davidic History & Folklore

The Book of Genesis provides a time-line, from the Creation with Adam & Eve in the Garden of Eden, through the death of Joseph in Egypt, probably around 1300 B.C.E. The narrative then picks up with the advent of Moses among the people, who beseeches Pharaoh to "Let my people go". Moses leads the people of Israel into the Negev desert and is succeeded by Joshua, who organizes them into a warring assault force to invade the villages of Palestine and conquer them, driving out and slaughtering the Philistines. As Israelites settle there, they divide themselves into tribes who are led by "judges" such as Sampson and Gideon. A leader named Saul emerges.

It's possible the Israelites were held captive in Egypt and this story is a memory of that, as told at the end of the book. However, the rest of the Genesis story is fable or folklore, devised to provide an explanation for many mysteries. There are similar stories in other cultures, but they are not meant to be taken literally. The invasion of Palestine recorded in Joshua may have some truth to it and the period of the Judges may have historical figures in mind with their stories and figures embellished. These were stories to provide self-identity and meaning to the origins of a people. But, to take them literally is unsupportable.

David & Solomon

Following the death of Saul in battle, David unites the tribes and leads them into the formation of the nation Israel. He ascends to the "Throne" of Israel in 1000 B.C.E. (Samuel 5). David is heralded for founding the United Kingdom and defeating the enemies of the Israelites. He is succeeded by his son Solomon, his son with Bathsheba, who continues to consolidate and strengthen the kingdom. Solomon is honored for his building of the Temple and palaces. Both had large harems and were ruthless with their enemies. Following the death of Solomon, the Kingdom divided, with Judah in the South (Jerusalem its capitol) and Israel in the North (Shechem its capitol).

The story of David and Solomon likely has some historical merit. As the Kingdom became established, it developed some of the usual institutions of a stable society, including the presence of scribes who were enlisted to record events (albeit to the benefit of the authorities, in this case, the priests, military leaders and governing officials). The record in the Book of Kings is more detailed and probably more contemporaneous than the more condensed story in Chronicles which was presumably written during the Babylonian Exile. But, in either case, there is no explicit social conscience, only accounts of personal transgressions and betrayal (e.g. Uzziah).

King Uzziah

The sixth chapter of Isaiah begins: "In the year that King Uzziah died….". It was a mournful year in Judah – for Uzziah had been a great and powerful leader and much-loved King, reigning from 783 B.C.E. to 742 B.C.E. Under Uzziah, Judah had made conquest of areas on both sides of the Jordan River but also gained a remarkable degree of economic and political stability. Bernard W. Anderson wrote:

"Unlike Israel, where swift economic changes led to the erection of an unstable social pyramid, Judah moved fairly smoothly from the simplicities of the old tribal order to the more advanced economy of town life, in the process, preserving an astonishing degree of social equality. True, the Northern Kingdom had no monopoly on evil. Judean prophets saw plenty of evidence that rapacious landlords were swallowing up the holdings of small farmers (Is. 5:8-10; Micah 2:1-2), that the rich were skimming the backs of small farmers (Is. 5:8-10, Micah 3:1-4), and that flagrant social injustices were smoothed over with a veneer of religious piety (chs.1:10-17). Nevertheless, the social order was relatively stable, and this stability – symbolized by the Davidic crown – is important to keep in mind…."

The Exile

Perhaps even more than the Exodus from Egypt, the period of the Exile in Babylon (587-538 B.C.E.) is the great watershed for the Hebrew people. While it was a traumatic experience for the Jewish people to be so far from home for almost fifty years, it provoked an outpouring of social cohesion that expressed itself in song, poetry and literary composition that constitutes what we now call the Old Testament. Without the Exile and the Return to the Holy Land, there might not be an identifiable Jewish people today for they would likely have simply been absorbed into the communities of the surrounding area.

The Return

With the Return from Exile in Babylon beginning in 538 B.C.E., the Jews reconstituted themselves in Palestine (as recorded in Ezra-Nehemiah) with the object of reconstructing the Jerusalem Temple as the center of their worship and community.

Daniel: Apocalypse

In the fourth and third centuries B.C., the successors of Alexander the Great divided up the territory east of the Mediterranean with the

Seleucids occupying Palestine and introducing Hellenistic culture to its people. This offended the Jews and they began to resist, as evidenced in the books of Esther and Daniel, even though the setting for these writings is earlier during the period of the Exile. Both are stories of collaboration and resistance.

The Bible

The Bible is commonly treated as a monolith of God's instruction to modern man while the timing of the books is treated as irrelevant. In point of fact, the Old Testament evolved over a period of hundreds of years and was composed by a variety of authors and assembled much later. The writings were done between 850 and 200 B.C.E. and finally assembled and canonized by a gathering of rabbis at the Council of Jamnia in 90 A.D. For the Jew, the basic scripture that was read regularly in the Temple and Synagogue was the Pentateuch or Torah, the first five books of what we now call the Old Testament. But, the Pentateuch contains not only mythical history. It consists of law in Exodus and Deuteronomy, genealogy in Leviticus and tribal census information in Numbers. Even in Genesis, there are multiple authors whose material has been commingled such as the dual stories of the Creation and the duplication stories of the Flood (just how many pairs of animals?).

For Christian communities, the Old Testament as we know it did not exist before the third century A.D. and the New Testament was not canonized until about the same time. In earlier years, there was no Bible, only various documents, some of which were well circulated but were not included in the authorized Canon when it was assembled years later. References to the Scriptures or to the Gospel did not apply to the Bible (it did not yet exist) but to the traditionally accepted messages that were later encompassed in the Biblical literature. Manuscripts were hand copied until the invention of the printing press a little more than five hundred years ago. There was no Bible in the form that we know it, just manuscripts, some of which were complete, most of which were not complete texts of the Bible.

So, the printing press wasn't invented until the middle of the fifteenth century A.D. Before that time, there were two methods of passing stories on from one generation to another: by oral communication and by handwritten manuscript on parchment. Oral tradition in all cultures was the far more common method of passing information on from one generation to another. What is remarkable is how consistent oral tradition was with the archeological record we are uncovering today, regardless of the culture. At the same time, oral tradition adds information that we can only regard as legend. Thus, Abraham, Jacob, Moses, Joshua, even David and Solomon may be fictional figures – or historical figures around whom storytellers wove legendary tales that illustrated a moral point or instituted a commemoration (such as Passover). In any case, these stories were transmitted orally from generation to generation for many years until they were eventually written down on papyrus or parchment by hand, then copied with the usual mistakes – and interpolations - that copiers normally make.

Before we go further, let's give a few dates as commonly accepted reference points. We cannot give a date for Abraham since he, even if he was a historical figure, is shrouded in the mists of time. Moses and the Exodus (for which there is no Egyptian record) are generally thought to have occurred around 1200 B.C.E. The most solid date we have is for King David who occupied the throne of Israel beginning in 1000 B.C.E. After a succession of kings and the separation of Israel and Judah, the Assyrian conquest of Israel (the northern Kingdom, with its capital in Samaria) is thought to have occurred in 722-21 B.C.E. and the Babylonian Exile of the people of Judah (the southern kingdom, with its capital in Jerusalem) took place around 587 B.C.E. The Return of the Jews, following the Exile, is dated around 538 B.C.E. under Cyrus the Great of Persia. The restoration of the Temple in Jerusalem occurred immediately after this with its dedication in 515 B.C.E.. It was destroyed again under the Romans in 70 A.D. These are all pivotal dates to know as references to the composition of the various parts of the Biblical literature.

Whatever existed prior to 722 B.C.E., most of what we know now as the Old Testament was written and collected during the years of the Assyrian and Babylonian Exile (721 – 538 B.C. E.) when it was important to unify the Hebrew people and give them a common tradition. (A few books, such as Daniel and Esther were written after the period of the Exile.) The Torah, the Dietary prescriptions, and the rituals (e.g. circumcision) were part of that unification process. Much was written during that period – Psalms, Proverbs, Song of Solomon, the prophetic materials, even the later histories of the kingly progression – and preserved after the years of Exile. Never was there an explicit Jewish canon, just the reading of the Torah and whatever else seemed appropriate in the Jewish community. The Old Testament canon was not completely established for Protestants until the early 19th century with the publication of the British editions of the Bible. To this day, there is no agreement on what the canon consists of since Catholics and others include books known at the Apocrypha.

There is also a difference in the order of the Old Testament books among the various traditions: Roman Catholic, Orthodox and Protestant. The books are also not in chronological order, especially with the prophets. Genesis through Habakkuk are considered historical books although the first five books (the Pentateuch) are deeply rooted in the mythical past and it is only with Joshua that somewhat reliable history begins. There is Wisdom literature (Psalms, Proverbs, Ecclesiastes, Job, Song of Solomon) that most likely dates from the time of the Exile, the many books of the prophets, and finally the post-Exilic books of Daniel and Esther.

Read Genesis, and you will see that it is composed of a series of stories which were undoubtedly transmitted by oral tradition long before they were written down. Some even bear similarities to stories found in other cultures. These were stories of a primitive people seeking a unifying heritage, a sense of their origin. Literal truth was irrelevant although it is remarkable how much of historical accuracy was preserved, but this is not unique to Hebrew culture.

Consider the various points of view expressed in the Biblical literature. The Book of Daniel and the Book of Revelation fall into the category of Apocalyptic literature, expectations of future cataclysm. On the other hand, there is the Book of Psalms which is a collection of laudatory poetry and the Song of Solomon which is completely hedonistic. The Book of Esther does not even mention God but rallies Jews to honor their nationalistic roots. Jonah, in contrast to many of the other books which vilify the enemies of the Jews, implores the people of God to evangelize the hated Assyrians. Even within books, you get different perspectives, as in Isaiah where at least two different writers exhort the People to repent (chs. 1 – 39) and renew themselves (chs. 40-66). At some later time, these various writings were collected into a common Book of literature despite their internal differences but as a testament to honor the common history of the People.

Likewise, there are different points of view expressed in the New Testament, both between the Gospel writers as well as among the authors of the canonized Epistles. Other gospel literature recounting the life of Jesus circulated in the first and second centuries but, because of the unorthodox perspectives presented, was omitted from the New Testament canon.*

*See the books of Bart Ehrman: *The Lost Scriptures, Misquoting Jesus*, etc.

My point is not to discredit the Bible, although I may be undermining your interpretation of the Bible. My purpose is to help you to see the Bible for what it really is: the literary record of a particular people assembled over many years to give them a corporate identity. This was most crucial in the period of the Exile when they were separated from their homeland and even from one another in a strange environment. God gave them a sense of unity and purpose and a separate identity from those foreigners among whom they lived.

There were, however, different threads of the story. In a simplistic breakdown, prophetic traditions that can be found in the Old Testament literature, especially the Pentateuch, identifying various points of view. Looking objectively at the material, it is hard to reconcile the concerns of a Micah or Jeremiah with the militaristic stories of Joshua and Judges or the priestly prescriptions of Leviticus and Deuteronomy. That these various traditions and stories were assembled together into various books was the work of ancient scribes who collected these many traditions into books and documents and did some editing of their own. Although there were probably some manuscripts that date back to the period of the kings in the post-Davidic period, much of the Old Testament in the edited form that we read today dates from the period of the Exile or of the post-Exilic period.

What this tells us is that what we call the Old Testament was assembled and written over the course of several centuries by people who had diverse memories and stories to tell and who held to different perspectives, some optimistic, some morose, some focused on history, some devoted to ritual, some concerned about justice and moral behavior, some concerned about eternal salvation, others seeking the good life here and now. It is probably true that they were inspired by their vision of God, but that image of God differed among them. They even had different names for God (Elohim, YHWH, Adonai) and that God played different roles in the lives of the Hebrew people. It is hard to say that the Scripture was infallible, inerrant and unalterably true. It is a record of how people experienced God, not of God's unwavering hand.

THE HISTORY OF THE NEW TESTAMENT

The New Testament is something else again. There is nearly a 400-year interval between the time of the last Old Testament book (Daniel) and the first writing found in the New Testament. Most scholars agree that the Crucifixion of Jesus occurred sometime around 33 or 34 A.D. but the first written record (a Pauline letter) found in the New Testament dates from about 65 A.D. One of the letters of Paul, and the earliest Gospel, that of Mark, dates around 80 A.D., nearly 45 years after the Crucifixion, a long time for a story with quotations and public and private events to be written down with accuracy. In fact, the four Gospels do not always agree and tell differing stories. The Gnostic (first three) Gospels are similar but also contain differences with the fourth Gospel, John, telling a very different story, especially in regard to the Crucifixion. Matthew and Luke tell different stories in regard to the Nativity. If one argues that the hand of God is guiding the Gospel writers, this is a problem. But, if one understands that oral tradition plays a part in transmitting information from one generation to the next, what we have is what one would expect: variations in the accounts.

Among the letters written to different churches, we have some that are authentically from the hand of Paul and some that are supposedly written by Paul (and James and John) that were not written by the authors to whom they are attributed. That does not make them worthless but simply means that the authors were attempting to claim a higher level of legitimacy for them than they would otherwise have had in the churches to which they were sent. Read them with an analytical mind and you will see that they represent different points of view.

What we are contending, therefore, is that the Biblical materials, whether in the Old or New Testaments, originated in oral tradition for years before they were written down – and in that time, they were influenced by then-current events, modified to reflect the personal biases of the tellers, rounded out to make them more meaningful, and embellished for dramatic effect. In a variety of contexts, oral tradition has been found to convey information with little change in historical fact from generation to generation. Nonetheless, modifications crept in. We can view these stories and narratives as the work of people inspired by God but not dictated by God as some would purport. The earliest documents we have were written by hand and passed on in handwritten manuscripts for generations until the invention of the printing press, more than a thousand years later. In the meantime, errors, edits and variations were incorporated into the books of the Old and New Testaments by scribes and it was the job of the translators, even the King James translators, to decide which texts were closest to the original. Even now, there are disputes, where there are differences, over which texts are the most authentic.

THE BIBLE: PERSPECTIVE

Read the Bible without preconceptions, as though you knew nothing about it and that it was something new. How would you regard the stories of Miracles in the Old Testament such as the Creation of man and woman, such as Moses parting the sea in the flight from Egypt, such as Noah, the Ark and the Flood, such as Daniel in the Den of Lions? How would you regard the command of God to the Israelites to slay the Philistines? What would you make of the stories of Samson & Delilah and David and Bathsheba? What would you think the prophets were trying to do? Then, looking at the Gospels, how would you interpret the Miraculous cures performed by Jesus – or the intent of his teaching?

What is so interesting is that what we have built over the past two thousand years is a religion and a church that Jesus never envisioned. Take a look at the Gospels. They report a Jesus who travelled about in Palestine healing people, admonishing hypocrites, teaching responsibility to others, telling parables and anticipating The End in a very short time. He gave no thought to establishing a church (let alone a "Christian nation"), paid little attention to ritual or vestments of rabbinic officials, was not interested in lasting structures, and doesn't even seem to be interested in theology. His focus was on the people of Judea that he met at the time. He may have been smart, but he was a simple man with simple. basic ideas for the common people. He showed great compassion for the weak, poor, sick and downtrodden. He didn't even attempt to lead a social movement but just to get people to rethink who they are and how they can be servants of one another.

When we look at the Bible without preconceptions, it becomes quite a different book and no longer a holy fetish but a chronicle of many different types of literature that was assembled not chronologically, not topically, not very coherently – but rather randomly. They are not all even about God (viz. Esther). You can reassemble them to read history. You can read them for ethical judgments about the Jewish people and the Kingdoms of Judah & Israel. You can even read them for beautiful prose and poetry. But, for coherence about the Jewish heritage, you need the supplemental writings of the rabbis.

History

It is hard to know when the first narrative material was written down after a lengthy period of oral transmission, but it probably occurred around the time of David when an organized priesthood was established and the period of disorder was close to an end. What was written among the various types of material is also unknown, although it was probably fable combined with historical material. The Law was likely first produced in written form around the time of David when priests desired some religious order and civil authorities wanted some consistency in legal prescriptions.

The Morality of the Bible or Moral Obligations

In any modern sense, much of the writing of the Old Testament fails in its attempt to convey a message of peace and civil community, Slavery is an accepted practice, although there are legal prescriptions as to how slaves are to be treated. There are prescriptions for killing those who commit certain offenses (including the cursing of one's parents). There are aggressive encounters re: the invasion of Palestine, in which the Israelites are instructed to kill and destroy, even commit genocidal acts against the Philistines. There are justifications for stealing and confiscating property from the enemies of the Israelites.

But, then there are the prophets who preach the importance of justice among the people. The wealthy who exploit the poor are condemned. There are authors, such as the author of Jonah, who encourage a positive approach to the Assyrians in Nineveh. And, then, there are the consolations for hardship, temptation and evil provided in the Book of Psalms.

The fact is that there is no consistency, at least in the Old Testament, for what is moral or immoral, justified or prohibited. "Fearing God" or doing the Will of God can be defined in many different ways. The best that can be said is that the Biblical literature provokes one to consider seriously what is moral (right) and what is immoral (wrong). But, to think that the Old Testaments offers a prescription for living piously or correctly is unfounded. For the Christian, the only guide is to follow in the footsteps of Jesus of Nazareth.

The Prophets

Beginning with Nathan, the prophet who confronted King David for his adultery with Bathsheba and his scheme to have her husband Uriah killed, there is a line of prophets who lived over a period of several centuries and who called both individuals and the nations of Judah and Israel to repent of their sinful and unjust ways. The prophets stand as a counterpoint to the apologists for the royal houses of Judah and Israel and to the priestly forces who argued that the religious ceremonial practices were a sufficient placating of the deity. Their concern was more with justice and righteousness rather than with ceremonial religious practice. In the words of Amos, "Let justice roll down like waters and righteousness like an ever-flowing stream" (Amos 5:24).

Jesus of Nazareth: The Quest for the Historical Jesus

His name was Jesus of Nazareth, not Jesus Christ. "Christ" is the Greek word for Messiah (and the meaning of Messiah is "anointed one"). To talk about Jesus Christ is to say that you regard Jesus as the long-awaited Messiah for the Jewish people. It is a testimony of faith, not a name. When "Jesus Christ" is used by a secular source such as a newspaper, it is being misused and is a rude imposition on those who are not Christians.

Read the Gospels without preconceptions as to who Jesus is. The picture the Gospel writers give of Jesus is that he clearly has an expectation of the End of the World - the Apocalypse – in a short time into the future and expects his followers to be prepared for it. In the Gospel of Mark, the first of the gospels to be written, he is the healer who cures people of their ailments. He has great compassion for the unfortunate as well as for adulterers and sinners. He shows contempt for hypocrites, authoritarians and those who prey on the poor and downtrodden. He is certainly not hyper-religious but simply adopts the religious attitudes of his day. He has great disdain for those who wear their religion on their sleeves but fail to show any regard for others in their daily practice.

The effort to recover the historical Jesus has gone on for many years now and there is a tendency to make him into the figure you want him to be. So, he has been identified with the full range of human personality traits, as a crusading warrior. a religious authority, an unrelenting prophet, a storyteller to children, a meek and pale wimp. Did he intend to found the religion that claims him as its progenitor? Or was he just trying to introduce some compassion and caring into the local culture of his time? I once asked a clergyman if he thought Jesus was a Pacifist and he replied that that was how he saw him. And, that is how I see him. But, you may disagree and you may be right. What Jesus would say in various situations, I can't say. But, one thing is clear. He was focused on the morality of human behavior, what today we call ethics.

There were numerous accounts of the life of Jesus, some of them with very different interpretations of his life, what he taught and who he was. The four gospels that were incorporated into the Bible represent a particular interpretation that is regarded as orthodox – but even they show some differences in interpretation and in his sayings. They were written many years after the Crucifixion and there were obvious embellishments and elaborations. What Jesus really said is often the subject of inquiry. Recently, The Jesus Project attempted to separate out sayings that are considered authentic from those that are dubious. You can read about this effort in *The Five Gospels*, by Robert W. Funk et al.

It is estimated that the Crucifixion took place in or around 32 A.D. In the forty years that transpired between then and the writing of Mark, the first Gospel, the remembrances of Jesus' life and sayings were primarily by oral transmission. There is a document, presumably of Jesus' sayings, now called Q (for Quelle), that was used by the authors of the Gospels of Matthew and Luke. There is no telling when it was written but it was likely several years after the Crucifixion. The problem is that what is remembered changes with time and telling. Think back thirty or forty years to remember events in your life – and consider how accurate you are in your recall.

We know of Jesus only through the Gospels, written by men who never knew him in the flesh and only recounted stories they were told by others. To what extent the figure of Jesus was inadvertently distorted by the Gospel writers we can only conjecture. Nonetheless, the figure of Jesus has been selectively portrayed in many different ways, from a meek and mild wimp to a bold, courageous and arrogant revolutionary. Though he is seen as a pious religious figure, the truth is that he dissented from the religious practice of the time, was contemptuous of the Temple priests and was more concerned about issues of justice and righteousness than with religious practice.

The trauma of his Crucifixion caused his followers to band together and to see him in a new way, as a fulfillment of Messianic prophesy. In the period between his Crucifixion and the writing of the Gospels, the memory of Jesus took on new dimensions. He was elevated to the Godhead and the prophetic aspects of his life in which he came into conflict with the religious and political authorities were downplayed, though still present in the Gospel material.

All of Paul's writings were likely written before the Gospels and reflect the theological development that took place in the intervening years. The Gospels, especially John, incorporate that theology which was developed over time and was heavily influenced by Paul. Other views of Jesus and theological ideas were floating about – but the Pauline view prevailed.

There is one thing we can say about Jesus, though, and it is consistent with his expectation of the End. Jesus was what we would today call an Ethicist. He was concerned with how people thought, behaved, acted and related to others. And, it is this concern with ethics that is important for those who profess to follow him.

What is so interesting is that what we have built over the past two thousand years is a religion and a church that Jesus never envisioned.

Look at the Gospels. They report a Jesus who travelled about in Palestine healing people, admonishing hypocrites, teaching responsibility to others, telling parables and anticipating The End in a very short time. He gave no thought to establishing a church (let alone a "Christian nation"), paid little attention to ritual or vestments of rabbinic officials, was not interested in lasting structures, and doesn't even seem to be interested in theology. His focus was on the people of Judea that he met at the time. He may have been smart, but he was a simple man with simple. basic ideas for the common people. He showed great compassion for the weak, poor, sick and downtrodden. He didn't even attempt to lead a social movement but just to get people to rethink who they are and how they can be servants of one another.

The Acts of the Apostles

The first years of the Christian movement are recorded in the Book of Acts, culminating with the missionary travels of Paul the Apostle. The focus of the book is the establishment of a Christ-centered world view and the effort to spread the Gospel. It downplays the diverse views of the Christian communities and completely ignores the disciples except for Simon Peter, even so leaving Peter in chapter 15 to focus on the travels and message of Paul, a self-appointed apostle. Apart from the activities of the Christian community to attend to its own needs and those of widows (Acts chapters 3 & 5), the focus is on winning believer converts rather than to provide for the welfare of non-Christians or to address the ills and injustices of society.

Paul & the other New Testament Writers

Under Paul, Christianity became a completely religious movement and abandoned not only any political/social perspective, it even abandoned the social thinking embodied in Jesus' message. Paul seems to know nothing about the life and ministry of Jesus, only speaking of his Crucifixion and Resurrection and what that means to him. Paul's morality seems to be confined to the responsibility Christians have for one another and the purity of their own behavior. To the extent that Christians have a responsibility to the wider community, it is to "evangelize" them.

Revelation

The Book of Revelation, written by a Christian named John on the Island of Patmos, late in the first century, reflects on the growing persecution of Christians with a message of encouraging steadfastness with the expectation that Jesus will come soon at the end of time. Again, it is looking inward for the faithfulness of the Christian in the light of persecution all around – and promising a day of victory. There is no expectation of an orderly and humane society – until God/Christ comes to rectify all things. The imagery is all religious and allegorical and reflects the troubled times in which the early church was trying to survive.

Apocalypticism

The idea about the end of the world is not new and originated independently in different cultures. The Book of Daniel is considered apocalyptic literature for it forecasts, in Daniel's dreams, a time of tribulation, followed by an end of time. According to the Gospel writers, Jesus himself expected an end of time in the not too distant future, although his words may have been misunderstood, instead saying that each person must face up to the reality of his/her mortal end.

Jesus frequently talked about the nearness of the Day of Judgment and the Kingdom of God. We usually think of the warnings as Jesus expecting an immanent Parousia – or end of time. Some scholars believe that Jesus expected an end game such as is described in the Book of Revelation as envisioned by John on the Island of Patmos. Others believe Jesus' used the concept of the Kingdom or of the Parousia to warn people to get their lives in order and their priorities straight before their lives were complete. Certainly, the idea of the Eschaton prevailed in the early church. No doubt, the Gospel writers give support to this idea in their accounts of the teachings and message of Jesus.

Nonetheless, it became a common belief in the early church that the end was coming and one needed to be ready. Of course, the Book of Revelation contains an extensive forecast of the Apocalypse that forms the basis of the common belief that there will be an end of time with a final judgment. There are those, however, who understand the Book of Revelation as metaphorical for the dire situation that Christians found themselves in at the beginning of the second century A.D. and John's message to be faithful despite the tribulation all around them.

Announcements that the world is coming to an end have cropped up steadily over the centuries, with false mentors leading their followers to mountaintops to await the return of the Lord at a specific time. Jesus didn't do that.

If you're still reading this, the Parousia (or Second Coming) hasn't happened yet and probably won't for many years to come, if ever. It's an aberration that won't go away, however. Rather than being the result of a Biblical forecast, it is more likely to occur, at least within the foreseeable future, as a result of a man-made cataclysm, such as a nuclear holocaust, a population explosion leading to famine and war, or an environmental miscalculation and catastrophe. So, the threat of an Apocalypse should not be dismissed out-of-hand. But, the threat to our world is not due to some heavenly intervention but to a catastrophe that is within the ability of humans to control. Perhaps that would be the ultimate heavenly Judgment.

The Truth of the Bible

Evangelicals start with the premise that the Bible is the "Word of God" rather than a discovery of whatever truth it contains. Billy Graham used to say: "The Bible says...." as though the Bible should be given unquestioning authoritative acceptance and that it is a uniform vessel of truth, undifferentiated in its content and sourced from the same Author.

It is inductive reasoning (invalid) to assume that the Bible has a single point of view, that it contains a uniform message and that it is divinely authored or even inspired by a controlling force. Inductive reasoning is false logic and begins with a premise that is unsubstantiated.

Is the Bible TRUE in all of its history and in all of its prescriptive sayings? Is the Law it dictates in Leviticus and elsewhere eternally and universally inviolate? Are the quotations compatible with one another? So, please look at the Bible and understand how it was composed and assembled, who wrote the books of the Bible and why and when the books were written and what were the circumstances of its composition. Then we can decide how Holy it is and to what extent it could be a source of guidance and inspiration for our lives.

In Ecclesiastes, for example, the writer says "Vanity of vanities, all is vanity…" something that hardly squares with the purposeful attitude of Paul and his contemporary evangelists. Let's see what the Jewish experience was before the advent of the Christian era and consider how the Old Testament came to be. Let's look at Jesus and see the man who really walked the roads of Palestine before the legends crept in. We will view the early Christian era to consider the distortions that took place. And, let's look at worship practices today and see how meaningful they are. And, let's look at what a meaningful Christian life could be in the modern world.

It is hard, then, to claim that the Bible is literally true in every respect. In fact, Biblical contradictions, competing accounts of events and different perspectives and philosophies (viz, Job, Psalms, and Micah) reveal it as more of a compendium of different viewpoints than as a monolithic statement of divine thought and dictation.

Oral Tradition and Transmission

As with the narratives passed down in many other cultures, for centuries or millennia, the stories of the Old Testament were transmitted by being told orally by one generation to another. Some stories were forgotten while others were added to fit in with the cultural milieu of the time.

In the telling, meaningful elements were infused into the narrative while those of less relevance or importance were discarded. The earliest written forms of the narrative likely go back to the time of David, around 1000 B.C. and were produced by scribes with varying points of view. There were Priestly narratives that emphasized the Law and the ritualistic elements of Hebrew worship. With the establishment of the royalty, there were the writers who emphasized and justified the royal aspects of the Jewish state. Even later came the Prophetic writers and scribes who introduced judgmental elements into the narrative of Hebrew society. Oral narrative continued to play a role that was gradually diminished by the written record.

The History of the Old & New Testaments

Give the Biblical books a break rather than making assumptions about what they are and where they came from. Consider them new-found writings that you are going to explore, just as you would any ancient documents. Consider what the material says and evaluate its contents in an objective manner, without preconceptions. It is literature from an earlier age, positing a pre-scientific worldview and reflecting the thoughts and preconceptions of an earlier time, reflecting various political and social biases of the authors. Some were mere poets, others were defenders of the monarchy, others were priests and religious authorities, some were early historians and others were simply storytellers. They did not all come from the same time and, thus, reflected the political and social situations of their day. Some were critics of the socio-political environment in which they found themselves, others were more complacent. They came with different concerns and viewpoints: contrast the pessimism of the author of Job with the Psalmists' assurance that the righteous will be rewarded (Psalm 23). Obviously, the writers of the Biblical material were educated and literate, in contrast to the vast majority of people who were uneducated and non-literate. But, they did not all agree, and arguments can be found within the books of the Bible, in both Old and New Testaments. You just need to look.

Moral Obligations: The Morality of the Bible

In Western culture, we have grown up with this God who would lead us in the "paths of righteousness". The Old Testament is dominated by stories that seem to carry a message with a moral sensitivity, usually with Israel (and later Judah) in the favored position. If these stories are read from the perspective of the evolution of religious thought, they coincide with other religious traditions. The Creation myth explains the origin of humans, their world and their society. The Flood myth explains historically experienced disasters. The Tower of Babel story explains the diversity of language. The monotheistic God is derived from a time of multiple gods (the plural Elohim is used as a name for God). God is a tribal God for the Israelites, leading them into battle, as opposed to the gods of the pagans. Only later does Yahweh (YHWH) become a God for all nations (as in Jonah). Only later, with the prophets, does God become a God of justice and righteousness. The Hebrew understanding of God evolved over the years.

It is clear, as a tribal God, that God was leading the Jews not only on a journey out of Egypt but also into a land already occupied by other peoples and seizing that land from those people. When invading villages such as Jericho and Ai, the Chosen People embark on a scorched earth campaign, killing not only the warriors but also, under the direction of God, the women and children of those villages. This is what we would expect of a marauding band of vagabonds but not of a holy people of God.

With the prophets, however, a semblance of justice is introduced. Nathan challenges King David, not only for his adultery with Bathsheba, but, more importantly, for his instigation of the death of her husband, Uriah, David also initiates cleansed-earth activities against his enemies and his son Solomon does likewise. Three hundred years later, Jeremiah calls the nation to repentance for its crimes and then there is Amos who demands "Let justice roll down like waters and righteousness like an ever flowing stream." Still, the historical books of the Old Testament endorse a tribal god who leads his troops into battle and blatantly endorses the special character of Israel as 'the Chosen People".

It always seemed to me that Christian faith embodied the highest ethical standard and moral system that could ever be conceived – one that embraced respect for all people, enhancement of human dignity, truth, honesty, justice, forgiveness, righteousness, civil rights, civil liberties and compassion for others.

Yet, you find in the Old Testament acts, including genocide, that are reputedly condoned by God. Women do not come off very well either, and slavery is regarded as an acceptable institution. And, you find throughout the centuries, atrocious acts against both non-believers and even Christians perpetrated by other Christians in the name of Jesus. Only a perverse soul like Pat Robertson would attribute a natural disaster, such as the hurricanes and destruction in Haiti and Puerto Rico, as a punishment by God for an alleged pact with the devil many, many years ago.

The Bible as the Word of God

So, what does it mean to describe the Bible as the Word of God when, so many human influences can be found in it, perspectives that are contradictory, and injustice that is tolerated if not embraced by some of the writers? Of course, there is also much material in the Bible that attests to an ethical code that is based on a theology of a just and righteous God, a God who cares for all people and who asks for adherence to an ethical standard.

6

THE SERMON ON THE MOUNT
(MATT. 5-7) & THE SERMON
ON THE PLAIN (LUKE 6)

hese sermons of Jesus are compilations of his preaching that
were apparently assembled at a later time and perhaps taken
from Q, a collection of Jesus' sayings. Matthew's version of the
sayings is longer and situated on a mountain (Gerazim? Carmel?) while
Luke's location is a plain (Sharon?). Matthew's version is better defined
from beginning to end while Luke's is more amorphous with some of
the sayings spread through the remainder of Luke's Gospel (chapter 6).
Note that there is no recorded "sermon" in the Gospel of Mark (and
no parallel sayings either). Mark's Gospel is the earlier Gospel that
both Matthew and Luke used (as well as Q) in order to compose their
own Gospels. The omission of the 'sermon' suggests that Mark did not
have the advantage of Q's collection of sayings but Matthew and Luke
did. John's Gospel has no parallel sayings whatsoever that duplicate
Matthew 5-7.

Nonetheless, the Sermon represents the core ministry and concerns
of Jesus and, in particular, his compassion for, and sensitivity to, the
people. That part of the Sermon we call the Beatitudes suggests his

identification with the poor and downtrodden, for those who have lived lives of sorrow and hardship and his encouragement of their faith.

THE BEATITUDES (MT. 5:3-12; LK. 6:20-23)

The Beatitudes are the most memorable part of the Sermon on the Mount, though they are abbreviated in Luke. They begin with "Blessed are...." Remember that Jesus was speaking to a crowd of people who lived in a land occupied by the Romans, overseen by a Roman Procurator and locally ruled by a "King" in a long line of privileged Herodians who brooked no dissention or criticism and who cruelly punished violators. The religious authorities were the privileged Sadducees, who controlled the Temple, and the Pharisees who tolerated no deviation from the Law of Moses. The people felt oppressed and sought relief.

With the Beatitudes, Jesus sought to give them comfort and a sense of worth – and extoled the qualities of righteousness, humility, mercy, personal strength, peacemaking and endurance against hatred. Matthew presents the Beatitudes as Jesus' opening remarks for his ministry, a prelude to his description of the fulfilling life, characterized by human responsibility.

You are the Salt of the Earth & the Light of the World (Mt. 5:13-16; Luke 14: 34-35)

Jesus is telling his followers that their lives have importance and a purpose. They have a role to fill in society – and toward one another. As Jews, they must live under Roman rule but, though they lack citizenship, they must see themselves as people responsible not only to one another but to the people of the world. They should hold their heads high and recognize their value and opportunity in the world.

Fulfilling the Law & the Prophets (Mt. 5:17-20)

It is never clear how Jesus regarded the Law as written in the Pentateuch (first five books of the OT). He observed its practices most of the time but deviated at others, even rejecting some of its harsher dictates. As fulfillment, he perhaps was saying the Law should be regarded flexibly and observed with respect to its intent to serve the people rather than the people to serve the Law. As for the prophets, he likely saw himself as one in the prophetic line and as one calling for justice and righteousness and the rejection of authoritarianism and hypocrisy.

Killing & Adultery and Divorce and Swearing an Oath & Revenge & Love (Mt. 5:21-48)

Here Jesus is pointing to attitude and motivation – and saying that anger and judgement with regard to another are just as ruinous to one's character as actually killing someone. The themes of forgiveness, love and reconciliation are introduced as contributing to one's better self and responsibility. They will be repeated again and again.

Jesus' recorded attitude with respect to divorce and adultery is both forgiving and harsh. It is likely that there is some interpolation here reflecting the views of the writer. Clearly, he wants to protect the position of the woman but the comments on committing adultery seem more judgmental that is otherwise characteristic for Jesus. That he would brand someone forever an "adulterer" because of a mistake is unlikely.

The comment on swearing an oath boils down to an issue of personal integrity. Don't promise anything you will later regret – but present yourself as an honest purveyor of integrity and truth.

On Retaliation (Mt. 5:38-42; Lk. 6:29-30)

Jesus recommends that "getting back at someone" (revenge) is just not worthy of human behavior and makes for an unworthy life. A generous and forgiving response is the better way.

On Love of One's Enemies
(Mt. 5:43-48; Luke 6:27-28, 32-36)

Jesus repeats the importance of reconciliation – and suggests that one will have a more worthwhile life as one who forgives. This is the ultimate essence of one's humanity. One could generalize from these comments that it is a person's attitude toward life and others that Jesus is seeking, not merely in one's immediate relations but in a more general attitude toward society. In today's environment of knowledge of the world and of rapid communication, one's social and political attitudes should be similarly compassionate, understanding and forgiving.

The Lord's Prayer (Mt. 6:9-15; Lk. 11: 2-4)

Again, Jesus focuses on looking outward with benevolence. In seeking God's will and the coming of the Kingdom ("Thy Kingdom come"), Jesus looks forward to a world in which understanding, and compassion will prevail. He then point to achieving a world that is characterized by what God wants, an ethical world ("Thy Will be done – on earth as it is in heaven.") – a world aspiring to perfection. "Forgive us our sins, as we forgive those who sin against us." Live a noble and responsible life and avoid succumbing to temptation. "Deliver us from evil" – both that which is done to us and that which we are wanton to perpetrate. That's the Lord's Prayer. Short and to the point – notably lacking any words of thanksgiving, something I've always wondered about since giving thanks was reported in several other utterances of Jesus.

The postscript "For thine is the kingdom, the power….." was added later and was not included in earlier manuscripts. It was added as Jesus was later regarded as a religious avatar.

Whether Jesus actually delivered The Lord's Prayer in the form as recorded by Matthew or Luke is something we cannot determine. Nonetheless, it serves as a model representing Jesus mode of reflection, hinting at our outward responsibilities and ethical conduct toward others.

False Piety (Mt. 6:22 – 7:14; various in Lk. 6, 11, 12, 13)

Hypocrisy abounds nowhere more than in pretense of being religious. Jesus despises hypocrisy wherever he encounters it. It abounded much in his day, even though in our time it is pervasive, especially among the purveyors of religion who draw huge crowds to their amphitheaters. Hypocrisy betrays that one is being dishonest and lacks integrity in one's dealings with others.

True Piety (Mt. 6:22-7:14); various in Lk. 6, 11, 12, 13)

The truly positive and rewarding life lies in single-minded commitment to helping others. Once again, Jesus deplores duplicity.

Beware of False Prophets (Mt. 7:15-23; Lk. 6:43-45)

It is easy to be misled from the truly responsible life. There are many who would like to deceive you for their own gain. For the sake of leading a responsible life, don't be gullible.

The Will of the Father (Mt. 7:24-29; Lk. 6:47-49)

It is not easy to lead a good, rewarding and wholesome life – and there are many temptations that would lead you astray. "The Will of the Father" can be understood as leading one's life in the highest, noblest and most selfless way conceivable. Consider your life as having such a noble purpose.

OTHER TEACHING FROM THE SERMON ON THE MOUNT

Following the Beatitudes, Matthew provides an assortment of Jesus' sayings as recollected over the years. Just how accurately they are remembered is difficult to say. However, for the most part, we can assume that they were consistent with Jesus' teaching and offer this commentary. (For a more enlightened discussion of the authenticity of these sayings, see *The Five Gospels*, Robert W. Funk et al.)

7

THE PARABLES OF JESUS – A SECULAR INTERPRETATION

The parables are not really religious in character but primarily about human behavior, what is good, what is bad and about the evolving world (i.e. the Kingdom of heaven). The problem is that we have trouble knowing just how accurately the parables were recorded. There weren't reporters standing around with note pads, jotting down his remarks in shorthand to be transcribed later. Those remarks considered important were remembered and recorded later, some perhaps correctly, some not so well. Oral statements are remembered if they are consistent with what one already believes, perhaps some that are innovative and striking, others morphed into what one prefers, and others completely disregarded. The scribe is in control.

If there are two or more scribes, perhaps they can confer at a later time and come to an agreement as to what was said. That being said, there are general themes that seem to have been constant with Jesus – so the individual parables and teachings that fit in to those themes could be said to be "authentic", at least in a general sense.

What is peculiar with the Gospel of John – and why it could be relegated to lesser status than the Synoptic Gospels – is that, although the Synoptics say that Jesus taught in Parables, John contains none of them. If Jesus taught that way, why does the Gospel of John not report them? It suggests that John's Gospel is more of a theological reflection than a real recounting of Jesus' life and ministry.

THEMES OF THE PARABLES

The themes of the parables can be categorized in this way:

1. You have been entrusted with certain abilities and talents. Make the most of what you have been given. Use them well and wisely – to live responsible and worthy lives, helping others with the things they need. (The Pounds, the Talents, the Salt & the Light, the Sower).
2. The Pious Priests, Scribes and Pharisees are undeserving. The good will be separated from the bad. (The Good Samaritan, the Wicked Tenants, the Marriage Feast, the Net). Beware of hypocrisy, especially religious hypocrisy.
3. There are important values to embrace. Be wary of seeking money and wealth. It can consume you. (The Unmerciful Servant, The Rich Fool).
4. A small amount of good works will mushroom into great things. (Salt & Light, the Sower, The Seed Growing Secretly, the Weeds, the Mustard Seed, the Leaven, the Hidden Treasure & the Pearl, the Good Samaritan, the Fig Tree, the Ten Maidens).
5. God advocates the obvious manifestations of Justice. (the Rich Man & Lazarus, the Unjust Judge).
6. There is reason to be optimistic about the future. The world will see better days ahead (heaven). (the Leaven, the Hidden Treasure & the Pearl, the Net).
7. The Importance of Forgiveness (The Unmerciful Servant).
8. The return or redemption of a person who has wandered into self-destructive ways is of particular importance and deserving of utmost gratitude. (Prodigal Son, The Lost Sheep & The Lost Coin).

9. The humbled will be exalted. They are the more deserving. (the Pharisees and the Publican, the Laborers in the Vineyard, the Two Sons, the Marriage Feast, Laborers in the Vineyard).

DEFINITIONS OF TERMS USED IN THE PARABLES:

The Kingdom of heaven

Jesus often uses the phrase "the kingdom of heaven" or "the kingdom of God" to point to human society as it should be, the way things ought to be, even the perfect world. It is not an otherworldly concept but the better way. In the parables, Jesus frequently says: "The kingdom of heaven is like …." to indicate his vision of what could be, the righteous, more humane way that we all should aspire to create.

The Righteous *(good)

The righteous are those who seek the betterment of all mankind, who have a keen sense of justice and fairness, and who live in such a way as to create such a world.

`The Unrighteous (haughty, evil)

The Unrighteous are those who foolishly seek a perverse way of living that fails to contribute to the betterment of human society and who, even, seek to take advantage of others or to do them harm.

Justice & Righteousness

Justice means fair and equitable treatment for everyone.

Those who forgive will be rewarded, if only in their own satisfaction that they are forgivers. Those who exhibit mercy toward others, especially those in great need, are those who deserve, and will be rewarded with, the most satisfying lives. Nonetheless, one doesn't do good for one's own satisfaction and benefit (although that is a by-product) – but for the good it does for others.

THE REASON AND PURPOSE OF THE PARABLES
(MT. 13:10-15; MK. 4:10-12; LK. 8:9-10)

What was Jesus' intent in speaking frequently in parables? Obviously, many of the parables he told were remembered by those who heard him – and were subsequently recorded by the Gospel writers. So, it is likely that Jesus wanted his teaching to be remembered and thought that could best be done with short, pithy stories. That's a pretty good reason for using parables as a teaching device. They were stories that made his listeners think, discuss and remember. The Parables are food for thought – but not all of his listeners were intent on discussing and thinking about them. Whether the Parables were remembered and written down as he wanted them to be is another matter. The parables are not always clear and do not always seem to have a point. In general, although they are clothed in religious language, they are commentaries about human behavior and the meaning and purpose of human life.

THE PARABLE OF THE SOWER
(MATTHEW 13: 1-9)

It's a simple message – and not necessarily a religious one. Jesus is trying to tell his disciples to be effective in what they do and say – and avoid frivolities. Just be sensitive to what you are doing. Don't waste your time and effort trying to accomplish meaningless things – or things that are fruitless where the possibility of their outcome is wasteful.

THE INTERPRETATION OF THE PARABLE OF THE SOWER (MT.13: 8-23; MK. 4:13-20; LK. 8:4-8)

It's interesting that Jesus needs to interpret the Parable since the interpretation is largely a restatement of the Parable itself. The point, of course, is that there are many things that can interfere with hearing and understanding the truth (i.e. the true purpose of living). What's important is to clear away those impediments and gain a true and righteous understanding of life's purpose. To do so is to achieve a rewarding and meaningful life.

THE PARABLE OF THE SEED GROWING SECRETLY (MARK 4:26-29)

Jesus frequently refers to the Kingdom of God – so it behooves us to understand what he means by "the Kingdom of God". It's a important question and it demonstrates Jesus' belief that there are better days ahead. Think of the context. The Romans occupy Palestine and their puppet ruler, Herod, is the regional satrap who is something of a tyrant. The Temple priests are nothing but exploiters of the people, constantly looking for ways to enrich themselves and their Judean rulers, the Herod family. So, Jesus is convinced this situation will not last and he looks forward to the future as "the Kingdom of God". The parable is intended to show that it will take time for this oppression to cease – but that it will happen. Plant the seeds of life now and, with patience, it will come to fruition. Just how that will happen he does not say – but the future is bright.

THE PARABLE OF THE WEEDS (MT. 13: 24-30, 36-43)

This parable talks about the presence of evil in the midst of a good and positive world. It's to be expected that things will not always proceed in a good and righteous manner. Just accept that fact. There are hardships ahead. But, the disciples did not get the drift of what he was saying, so they asked him about an interpretation of the parable.

The Interpretation of the Parable of the Weeds (Mt. 13:36-43)

Jesus is prodded to explain the parable and tells his followers that, despite troubles and wickedness, the good will prevail. So, do not lose heart. Continue to do good, support the good, persevere for the good. The bad things will be rooted out and destroyed but you will find reward in continuing to seek the just, the righteous, the good.

The Parables of The Mustard Seed & The Leaven (Mt. 13:31-33; Lk. 13:18-2)

Jesus suggests that small acts of goodness can blossom into wonderfully good results for everyone. The tiny grain of a mustard seed can grow into a magnificent tree. It doesn't take much of an effort to do a tremendous amount of good for others. Similarly, the leaven one mixes into dough can make a large loaf of bread. He encourages people to see what good they can do with such a small amount of effort.

Many years ago, Lloyd C. Douglas wrote *Magnificent Obsession*, a 1954 book which told the story of a Christian doctor who performs acts of kindness for people, especially the poor who could not pay him. He insisted that they not tell anyone about the things he did for them. It was based on this idea that each person is capable of a great deal that will help others with only a small amount of effort, that one should do this without a claim to fame and fortune which can only detract from the resulting good.

The Parable of the Hidden Treasure and the Pearl (Mt. 13: 44-46)

Again, Jesus emphasizes that good deeds have their own reward and that being selective about what you want in life can be the most beneficial and productive way to live your life. One's character is what is important, not the extraneous things that are worthless

THE PARABLE OF THE NET (MT. 13:47-50)

Again, Jesus suggests there are two ways to live one's life: a positive way and a negative way.

THE PARABLE OF THE HOUSEHOLDER (MT. 13:51-52)

Jesus is apparently saying that the old teaching has merit to it but that his teaching contains much that is new – and that you are well advised to respect both: the positive elements of past teaching (and religion) and the new understanding and interpretation that he is expounding.

THE PARABLE OF THE GOOD SAMARITAN (LK. 10:29-37)

Jesus turns to a more specific exhortation to what is human responsibility toward everyone. Samaritans were disregarded by Jews as apostates and despicable foreigners, even though they held to the Torah and traced their origins to the Exodus experience. Samaria, to the northeast, had its own Temple at Shechem and a separate worship tradition, though from the outside (e.g. by the Romans), they were also regarded as Jews. So, for the despised Samaritan to come to the aid of the beaten and offensive man who lay by the roadside was a deep act of selflessness, especially when the man was ignored by the priest and the Levite, paragons of religiosity, who passed on by.

In modern parlance, Jesus was encouraging his listeners to dismiss the temptation of intolerance based on ethnicity (in this case) and to offer brotherly assistance (compassion) where and when it is needed. In contrast to the attitude of the priest and Levite, the response of the Samaritan is true religiosity.

THE PARABLE OF THE LOST SHEEP
& THE LOST COIN (LK 15:1-10)

Again, Jesus is encouraging his followers to welcome back the wayward brother or sister. It is forgiveness and welcoming inclusion that are important, not punishment arising out of intolerance. It is such a contrast to the judgmental religiosity that arose again in Christianity and is an inevitable characteristic of humanity. Be happy for the person who is redeemed and recovers.

THE PARABLE OF THE RICH MAN
& LAZARUS (LK 16:19-31)

Jesus does not have much compassion for the wealthy who do not act mercifully toward those who are impoverished and suffer. His parable conveys his disregard for those who enjoy the pleasures and comforts of life and show no compassion for those who are poor and distraught. It is not the wealth per se that offends him, though he is anguished by the way wealth can impede the owner's righteous practice to aid the impoverished and to help them to recover. So, he uses the metaphor that matters will ultimately be settled. The righteous will be exalted and the unjust will be brought low. Justice will be achieved in the end.

THE PARABLE OF THE PHARISEE &
THE PUBLICAN (LK. 18:9-14)

This Parable is basic to Jesus' entire teaching. He once again finds the humble person who is aware of his faults more acceptable than the person who is so proud of his public standing and religiosity. If there's anything Jesus despises, it's false religion and egregious pomposity. He seems much more tolerant of human frailty than of narcissistic self-aggrandizement.

THE HYPOCRISY OF THE PHARISEES (LK. 16:14-15)

In this brief passage, Jesus again denounces the hypocrisy that often accompanies religiosity. The Pharisees are regarded by other men for their pretense of piety. In truth, such piety falls short of what is expected of honest people.

THE PARABLES OF THE GREAT SUPPER & THE MARRIAGE FEAST (MT. 22:1-14;LK. 14:15-24)

These are essentially the same Parables, told in slightly different form – but they convey what is essentially the same message: that those who accept the actual responsibility of living meaningful lives are the few who do not even have the advantages of others who fail in their lives to take up the right and true form of living.

THE PARABLE OF THE POUNDS/ TALENTS (MT. 25:14-30;LK. 19:11-27)

This is a rather startling Parable, where the servant who is careful about not risking his master's money is rejected for his caution. But, the Parable is not about money – but about the way one is expected to live his/her life. You can hoard or waste your gifts or you can go out and do some good for others. Even those who do just a little on behalf of others are expending some valued effort – in contrast with the person who makes no contribution to his community.

THE PARABLE OF THE UNMERCIFUL SERVANT (MT. 18:23-35)

Again, the Parable is not about the actual situation but is an analogy to the way we live and relate to others. Jesus encourages us to be understanding and forgiving but hates hypocrisy. Here, the forgiven servant fails to be merciful, even though he has begged for and received mercy. His failure to forgive another is deserving of contempt – and punishment. Jesus emphasized the importance of forgiveness in The Lord's Prayer where he emphasized the relationship between asking for forgiveness and the importance of forgiving others.

THE PARABLE OF THE RICH FOOL (LK. 12:13-21)

Here's another analogy to living one's life: it's who you are, not what you possess, that is important. When we concentrate our efforts and center our lives on what we acquire, we miss the point of living. What is the purpose of life? In Jesus' parlance, it's to be servants, neighbors and friends to others, not to build up our hoard of possessions.

THE PARABLE OF THE SERVANTS' WAGES (LK. 17:7-10)

The Parable seems a bit strange – but the point is to recognize one's humility when fulfilling one's responsibility. As in other teachings, Jesus suggests that doing the right thing is its own reward and not something to boast about.

THE PARABLE OF THE PRODIGAL SON (LK. 15:11-32)

The well-known Parable is about gratitude for the recovery of someone who has returned from a wayward life. The "lost" son is welcomed back by the father who is so pleased to see his son return. The brother is bitter because he has been dutiful and feels he deserves recognition for his faithfulness to his father. The father responds that "you are always with me", meaning that their bond is secure. But, the prodigal son was lost and the father had given up all hope for his return. But, now that he has returned, the father is overcome with joy.

The point Jesus is making is that recovery from lost hope is worth more than the ordinary fulfillment of duty.

THE PARABLE OF THE LOST SHEEP (MT. 18:10-14)

Here is a parable that is also reminiscent of the Prodigal Son – for it rejoices in the recovery of one who is lost but now is found. The Parable has to do with the importance of relationships and the recovery of one who has drifted away – or gone off the deep end – and now has returned or been found and recovered.

THE PARABLE OF THE DISHONEST STEWARD (LK. 16:1-13)

This is a difficult parable to interpret. Clearly, it is a kindness for the debtors that the steward decided to discount the debts of others, although he was trying to save his own neck in doing so – and it was also at his master's expense. But, the master commends the steward for his "prudence", perhaps meaning that the master was satisfied that he resolved his debtor problem. Jesus then concludes that "You cannot serve two masters, God and mammon." Was the steward serving the higher morality by discounting the debts? It's an ambiguous parable.

THE PARABLE OF THE UNJUST JUDGE (LK. 18:1-8)

Here's another tough parable to understand. Perhaps it's about forgiveness of the undeserving (and not about the judge at all). Perhaps it encourages those who are merciful to overlook the undeservedness of those who need forgiveness – and the willingness to be forgiving of them. Perhaps.

THE PARABLE OF THE LABORERS IN THE VINEYARD (MT. 20:1-16)

Again, the Parable seems to be at a disparity with a sense of justice. The laborers who worked the full day for an agreed upon wage now feel cheated since those who worked only an hour received the same pay. As in the Parable of the Prodigal son, perhaps this Parable also is about the importance of gratitude for whatever it is that one has – rather than for what might have been.

THE PARABLE OF THE TWO SONS (MT. 21:18-32)

This is a Parable about the difference between being Faithful and Faithlessness. He is speaking to the chief priests and the elders – and tells the story of the two sons. Despite saying he will not do what the father asks, the first fulfills his responsibility to his father; the other son fails, despite what he says. Jesus disliked hypocrisy intensely and the willful failure to fulfill what had been promised. He valued integrity, which the first son demonstrated by his doing what the father asked. The second son, by his irresponsibility, failed the loyalty he owed to his father. By telling this story to the religious authorities, he is suggesting that they do what they are chosen to do – to serve the people and not to control and take advantage of them.

THE PARABLE OF THE WICKED TENANTS (MT. 21:33-46)

This, also, is a Parable about Faithlessness. The tenants are entrusted with a mission and a purpose, which they fail to perform. The chief priests and Pharisees are put in the same position, failing in their purpose to serve the people. Jesus concludes: "This kingdom will be taken away from you." (Interestingly, the Temple was destroyed by the Romans about 40 years later – and never rebuilt.)

THE PARABLE OF THE FIG TREE (MT. 24:32-33; MK. 13:28-29; LK. 21:29-31)

THE PARABLE OF THE TEN MAIDENS (MT. 25:10-13)

These two parables are told in Jerusalem as Jesus nears the end of his ministry, just a day or two before he is about to be taken prisoner and led away to be tried before the Sanhedrin. He recognizes his teaching is offensive to the religious authorities and they would like to be rid of him. He tells these parables as a way of saying that his listeners need to be steadfast and faithful in seeing their lives as worthwhile and in carrying out their responsibilities to one another, to continue his teaching of fairness, tolerance, and care for one another and for all humanity.

THE PARABLES

So, you see, the Parables have little to do with religious or heavenly matters but are, in large part, how to fulfill one's life by living responsibly with others. Jesus hated hypocrisy; he hated saying one thing and then doing something else; he hated instances where promises were made and then those promises went unfulfilled.

Nonetheless, when reading the parables, remember that they were written down many years after Jesus ministry. During the period of oral transmission, they were undoubtedly modified in some inadvertent ways to reflect changing circumstances and the mind of the writer. Consider them in light of your knowledge of what Jesus was likely trying to convey to his disciples and followers.

8

OTHER TEACHINGS OF JESUS (RECORDED IN THE SYNOPTICS)

CLEANSING OF THE TEMPLE (MK. 11:15-19; LK. 19:47-48)

Jesus despises hypocrisy. The Temple is dedicated as a holy place for the reflection of the soul. It has been leased out for commercial purposes, for the making of money. The Sadducees ran the Temple as a way to make money from the religious devotion of the people – and this incensed Jesus so much that he began overturning tables. Such activity has persisted into the present. Luther was repelled by the sale of indulgences, not unlike Jim Bakker and other evangelists' activity in selling various kinds of products to unaware and believing people.

AGAINST THE PHARISEES (LK. 11:37-12:1)

The Hypocrisy of the Pharisees (Luke 16:14-15)

In these two somewhat different passages, Jesus tell the Pharisees that their emphasis on appearances is deceitful and betrays what is important: the inner, true person. It is the basic reality of who you are that is important, not the personage you present to the world. For all their outward pretense of religiosity, the Pharisees are basically hypocrites who pretend to be important figures in the community, but who neglect their real obligations to the people. The goodness and purity of the soul are what is important, not the outward show.

THE NATURE OF DISCIPLESHIP (MT. 8:18-22; LK. 9:57-62; LK. 14:25-35); DISCIPLESHIP

It is apparent, from the frequency that he talked about it, that Jesus wanted those closest to him to learn from him and to carry his message forward, his message of love and tolerance and common humanity. He recognized that his message contravened the accepted order of the day, whether it be the legalism of the Jewish authorities, the authoritarianism of the Roman pagan autocracy, or the self-centered parochialism of the common people. He knew the disciples would encounter resistance, even possibly danger. He knew there would be a tendency to veer off message by succumbing to the religiosity, represented by the Pharisees in Palestine and others elsewhere.

(A few years before he died in a Nazi prison, Dietrich Bonhoeffer wrote a very influential book called *The Cost of Discipleship*, the title suggesting that being a disciple of Jesus is never easy. It requires self-sacrifice and, perhaps, danger for being independent of powerful opponents. Discipleship requires commitment, integrity and perseverance – and risk, Not everyone can be a true disciple.)

Conditions of Discipleship (Mt. 16:24-28; Mk. 8:34 – 9:1; Lk. 9:22-27)

Again, Jesus makes the point that one's life, to be really human, must have a positive, wholesome purpose. The way of life he teaches is expressed as following him, even though it may entail some hardships (i.e. taking up one's cross). There are self-gratifying ways of living, but they gain nothing. In an apocalyptic ending to the passage, Jesus proffers that justice will prevail, expressed as the Father repaying every man for what he has done.

FEARLESS CONFESSION
(MT. 10:25-33; LK. 12:1-12)

Once again, Jesus encourages his followers to act courageously and not be fearful being honest with themselves, of telling the truth about the purpose and meaning of life, and of being servants of one another. Being honest about oneself may be cause for even some family disruptions and may not win general favor in the community, but seeking a deeper level of commitment and trust with others will be the better course of action.

SENDING OUT DISCIPLES
(MK. 6:6-13; LK. 9:1-6; LK. 10:1-16)

Fate of the Disciples (Mt. 10:17-25)

Jesus is sending out his disciples to spread his message of love, compassion, tolerance and truth, even among villages that are characterized by animosity with the Jews. He encourages them to rely on the generosity of those they meet along the way – and to present his message of personal wholeness and honesty and ethical behavior. They were told to help with healing and restoring. But, where they were made to feel unwelcome, they were simply to leave without argument. They have done the best they could.

Jesus does not wince at telling his disciples that truth telling has its risks. In challenging the hypocrisy and scheming, cheating, abusive, deceptive practices they will encounter, they will often find themselves in hostile territory. They will need wisdom, strength and courage to deal with these situations but need to remain strong in telling the truth. They may even suffer physical harm, be reviled and be rejected – but they are to persist. For, in the end, righteousness will prevail.

Division in Households
(MT. 10:34-36; MT. 12:25-37; MK. 3:28-30)

Here, Jesus faces up to the discord within families that his message may bring. Whether the Gospel writers got it right or not is not clear. What is Jesus talking about? Is it religious? Or, is it perhaps a social message – that family members may not appreciate a truthteller sticking his nose in where they feel it does not belong? Jesus was not averse to taking on the political and religious authorities for their hypocrisy and wrongdoing. Could it be that he realizes that family members may object?

Questions Concerning
Tribute to Caesar (MT. 22:15-22; MK. 12:13-17; LK. 20:20-26)

The Pharisees and partisans of Herod were trying to trap Jesus over the issue of tribute, thinking that he might dissuade some of his followers if he came down on the side of Herod's demand for tribute. Cleverly, Jesus throws the issue back to them, suggesting that one does have some obligation to government while at the same time having a responsibility to use money on behalf of the community (as one's obligation to God).

About Greatness
(MT. 18:1-4; MK. 9:23-27; LK. 9:46-48)

So, what does it take for a person to be great? Boasting is not the route to greatness. Even seeking greatness is not the route to take. It is humility and self-abnegation that fulfill one's personal purpose, that make one whole and full of life. We have seen the disparity in the political arena. Someone who truly wishes to serve the people he/she knows, feeling a sincere obligation to them, decides to enter a political race, sometimes even as a personal sacrifice, not to enhance his/her personal glory but to try to do some good for others. This contrasts with others who, for reasons of personal gain, enter politics for their own benefit, and are willing to sell their souls to other interests in order to do so. Cynics think all politicians are in the latter class. Not so. There are those who enter politics to benefit others.

ON HUMILITY (LK. 14:7-14)

Again, one of Jesus' themes is to express humility while, at the same time, recognizing one's self worth. One is well to regard himself/herself without exaltation, simply taking a modest station in life. Don't try to elevate yourself, he says. Let others do that for you. It is better to be raised up rather than to try to take a higher status in life than is appropriate – and from which you will be brought down. "Everyone who exalts himself will be humbled, and he who humbles himself will be exalted."

CAUSING SIN (LK. 17:1-4)

Jesus warns his disciples to be careful that they do not lead others into actions that are harmful to others (i.e. sin). Again, Jesus encourages his followers to take responsibility for the actions of others and to prevent them from making evil and harmful mistakes.

FORGIVENESS (LK. 17:3-4; MT. 18:21-22)

Jesus emphasizes the importance of forgiveness – and our responsibility to forgive others, even in cases of repeat offenses. In such instances, it is rare when there is real repentance – but it is what Jesus counsels. He suggests that indefinite grudges are harmful to the one who holds them – and that it is better to forgive and forget. In other words, Jesus wants people to understand that they need to be flexible about being wronged – that they share responsibility for one another and that they need to be more tolerant and understanding, if only for one's own sake. Otherwise, when you are the cause of someone else's wrongdoing – or you continue your anger with someone else, it is like a millstone around your neck. Seeking reconciliation with others is the better way than nursing a grudge where one's guilt and anger are in control and limit one's ability just to be a positive human being. Here, Jesus is talking about human character and one's ability to make a positive contribution to society and not for some heavenly reward.

COMFORT FOR THE HEAVY LADEN (MT. 11: 28-30)

The way of life that Jesus encourages his listeners to follow represents a wholesome fullness of life, a meaningful and fulfilling way of living. He asks them to take his yoke upon themselves, indicating that it may entail some hardship – but that, in the end, it will be the right way of living.

TEMPTATIONS (MT. 18:7-9; MK. 9:33-37; LK. 9:46-48)

Here Jesus rephrases his theme about living a fulfilling life. It is easy to be distracted from doing the right thing, pursuing your purpose and leading a fulfilling life. It's easy to be distracted by the pursuit of money, power and glory. Give up the distractions and be intent on improving the lives of those around you, a purpose that constitutes a meaningful life.

CARES ABOUT EARTHLY THINGS (LK. 12:13-24)

Once again. Jesus tries to clarify what is important in life: "A man's life does not consist in the abundance of his possessions." He is more concerned with the values one embraces, the attitudes one shows, the quality of the relationships one has, the concern, respect and love for one another,

THANKSGIVING (MT. 11:25-27; MK. 8:6; 14:23;LK. 10:21-22)

It is peculiar that, in the Lord's Prayer, the model for prayer, Jesus omits the feature of thanksgiving. There actually isn't much in the Gospels about giving thanks or thanksgiving, although there are several references when, before eating a meal, Jesus is reported to have "given thanks" – but there is no actual teaching about thanksgiving.

THE GREAT COMMANDMENT (MT. 22:34-40; MK. 12:28-34)

Intent on trying to trick him and perhaps to start an argument, Jesus is asked by a Pharisaic lawyer to name the greatest commandment. He responds by saying that one should love God – and his neighbor as himself. "On these two commandments hang all of the law and the prophets". He summarizes the basis of all of the commandments, simplifying them in the process and reducing their legalistic interpretation. It is certainly consistent with Jesus' other teaching, that one's devotion to God is shown by one's caring for one's neighbor. Without that compassionate demeanor for others, there is no devotion to God.

THE KINGDOM OF GOD (LK. 17:20-21)

The Parousia (Mt. 24:4-8; Mk. 13:5-8; Lk. 21:8-11)

As interpreted by the Gospel writers, Jesus seems to expect that the coming Parousia will come reasonably soon.

Here in Luke Jesus proclaims: "The kingdom of God is in the midst of you", revealing his contention that it is in the present, here and now, that people have their rightful place of living, that they need to pay attention to the NOW and not to a future payoff in an afterlife heaven.

Jesus' statements about the Kingdom of God are ambiguous. The

Gospel writers were fairly definitive in reporting that Jesus believed the Parousia (the coming of the Kingdom) was imminent. However, In Luke 21, he states that "the kingdom of God is in the midst of you", suggesting that it is the present accounting of each of us that is important, that living our lives in the present time is what will inaugurate the Kingdom of God for each of us.

DESTRUCTION OF JERUSALEM
(LK. 19:39-44)

Sign for this Generation (Lk. 11:29-32)

Jesus apparently saw that the political situation at the current time would eventuate in the destruction of Jerusalem (which actually occurred in 70 A.D.). He refers back to Jonah's warning to Nineveh, another city that was destroyed a few hundred years earlier. He wanted people to survive the catastrophe by being prepared for it. Once again, he suggests that the material world was not the center of our meaning but the world of values - and ethics – and humane relationships.

RESURRECTION (MT. 22:23-33;
MK. 12:18-27; LK. 20:27-40)

The question of Resurrection is posed to Jesus by some Sadducees who are hoping to trick him and discredit him among his followers. The Pharisees are those who believe in the Resurrection while the Sadducees do not. Which camp is Jesus in? Jesus sidesteps the question and concludes with a memorable statement: "He is not God of the dead, but of the living." Once again, Jesus deflects the issue of heaven and the afterlife and concentrates his attention of how people live their lives now, the meaning and purpose of life now and the value of relationships.

It is clear, in his parables and teachings, that Jesus is focused on how people live their lives in relationship to one another, not in their religiosity or their adherence to a set of rules – or even their financial or social success. He values truth and integrity, sensitivity, love and compassion, caring for the weak and distraught, and purposeful living. He is not parochial or doctrinaire – nor is he intolerant or bigoted. He does not aspire to more than his due. He simply wants to be a well-regarded teacher, encouraging people to honor the ethical values he represents. He bids people to follow in his footsteps.

9

CONCEPTS, IDEAS & DOCTRINES

A NOTE ABOUT WORDS: WHAT DO YOU MEAN BY THAT?

Just a note about words. Words have no substance in and of themselves. Just because there is a word used to represent something does not make that thing real and, yet, people often assume that something exists if there is a word for it. So, whether the word is ghost or dragon, heaven or angel or demon, it does not necessarily exist. A word represents an idea, not necessarily a reality.

GOD

The problem with our concept of God is that it is too limited – too fixated on our lives rather than upon the purpose we have in the world.

We often refer to the Kingdom of God with God sitting on His royal throne. We refer to God as Lord. That royal language is a holdover from a time when kings ruled countries and the political order was monarchical. We now live in a modern age when democratic forms of government are seen as less tyrannical, fairer, and more equitable and just. Would it not be more appropriate to think of God as more inclined to equity among people and more tolerant of diversity?

Imagine. Everyone has their own mental image of who God is. There are probably as many ideas of God as there are people in the world. No two people think of God in precisely the same way. So, our idea of God is captured by – and limited by – the way we think of God. But, God must transcend the way we think of God. – or God is not God. The theologian Paul Tillich used to speak of "the God beyond God", the God who is far beyond our conceptualization or ability to comprehend.

Many years ago, J.B. Phillips published a book titled ***Your God is Too Small*** in which he suggested that we need to expand our thinking about the way we envision God. Too easily, we think of God in human terms, as though God existed as a human writ large. In Medieval times, God existed in the clouds with his angels and cherubs all about. God was conceived of in the male gender – but that too was too confining. Slowly we are abandoning the male pronouns and recognizing that God must be beyond gender.

Consider the vastness of the universe. Modern day astronomy reveals to us that our planet is a minute particle of all of the mass in the universe, that there are billions of stars out there, many more massive than our own sun, and that they stretch out into far distances beyond the reach of our best telescopes and electronic detection devices – for billions of light years. This is God's domain – far greater than we could ever conceive – and the people on earth, all eight billion of us, are an infinitesimal fraction of that universe. The ancient Hebrews believed that God had entered into history, guided them into the Promised Land and fought battles on their behalf, until they, centuries later, succumbed in battle, first to the Assyrians and then to the Babylonians, because of their faithlessness, and were led away into captivity in Babylon. Their God was a god of minute occasions - and we face the same danger.

THE SUPERNATURAL

We live in a world of realities but there are many things we do not understand – yet. It is in the realm of what is not understood where we conjure up myths that superimpose themselves upon our lives. The Supernatural has a certain appeal for us – but, in this day, we understand life differently than did our forbearers who saw the Supernatural all around them in the form of ghosts, spirits and other mysterious events. Although there are still those who delve on the mysterious and are intrigued with non-natural explanations for events that are difficult to explain, the idea of the supernatural has been seriously eroded in the last few hundred years. Both rational and scientific explanations have displaced these primitive explanations for the mysterious.

FAITH & WORKS

From the time when we were children, we have heard that we must accept God – or Jesus – on the basis of faith. Commonly, the example of Abraham, being instructed by God to sacrifice his son Isaac, is used to justify that argument. As Abraham makes ready to kill his son, he demonstrates his faith in God – and his hand is stayed.

We know of fanatics who believe they have been instructed by God to commit some heinous act. They really believe they have been singled out to do something that is contrary to all reason, in contrast to a humanitarian act. Jihadists apparently have the terrible conviction that to destroy lives and property of infidels, even of their own people and fellow believers (though heretical), is their duty to God. Rather than contribute to human betterment and the improvement of life, they believe it is better to devote their lives to destruction.

Reason and common sense lead us to wholly different conclusions, that belief in God leads us to lives of compassion and creativity, to building up rather than tearing down. Reason has been propounded as in contrast to Faith, with Faith being the superior mode. Yet, Faith bears the liability to be whatever you want to make of it whereas Reason operates by some commonly acknowledged set of principles.

Reason tends to be cautious while Faith is more impulsive. Reason is more humane while Faith is more otherworldly and capricious. Reason bases its logic on knowledge while Faith tends to be more intuitive and independent of knowledge.

If Faith assumes an attitude of humility, it can be less self-righteous and arrogant than Reason. In that case, it is more humanitarian and selfless than Reason. So, perhaps the choice is not between Faith and Reason but rather to adopt an attitude wherein one tempers the other in a constructive way, to assume the best qualities of each.

CREATION & EVOLUTION

There is a church in my community that holds an anti-evolution conference every year and imports speakers who talk about the inner contradictions, the illogicality and the failures of the evolutionary idea. Of course, these speakers are not true biological scientists but experts in some other field (like electro-magnetics) or engineers or clergy from elsewhere. For whatever reason, they have an agenda that assumes that evolution and religious belief are inconsistent with each other – and their religious belief trumps science. Unfortunately for them, the vast majority of scientists in the field of biology not only base their work on the basic concepts of Darwinian evolution, they regard evolution as scientific fact (insofar as a scientist can posit any "fact"). For the Fundamentalist, however, there must be a line between other animals and homo sapiens, a line that demarks a qualitative leap from the animal kingdom to humans wherein God made man "in His image" and into whom He blew the "breath of life".

Not far from this church in Bozeman, there is a museum, the Museum of the Rockies, which harbors one of the finest collections of dinosaurs in the world. The museum's dinosaur exhibit is founded on the premise of evolution, wherein dinosaurs evolved over millions of years and then went extinct sixty-five million years ago, when a meteoroid from space smashed into the Yucatan and spread toxic dust and debris around the world. Except that the dinosaurs did not go extinct since a branch of the dinosaur kingdom survived in the form of birds who, in turn, evolved over the ensuing period of millions of years.

A million years is an extremely long period of time. According to anthropologists, humans appeared on the scene about 100,000 years ago, evolving out of more primitive primate forms that first appeared a million years ago. A lot can happen in a million years. A lot more can happen over sixty-five million years. There is no reason not to believe this progression. Consider how dogs have changed over the two to five thousand years of history when the Egyptians dominated the Middle East and left drawings of dogs in their time.

So, is there an inconsistency between evolution and a Christian view of life? And, if there is, which view should dominate and be accepted by us?

DEMON – SATAN – LUCIFER

The idea of demonic forces, including the personalized form of Satan or Lucifer, is only primitively conceived in the Biblical literature. It was part of the folklore of the time to personalize the hostile environment and to explain human psychological abnormalities. It was in the Middle Ages that a pantheon of demons and devils, witches and gargoyles, came to be part of a pervasive communal belief – and that one could be possessed of a devil or evil spirit.

EVIL, SIN & PUNISHMENT

The concept of Sin is a catch-all term, used for minor thoughts as well as horrific actions. Certainly, no one would equate a greedy impulse with the brutal torture of an enemy, yet both are "sins". There are sins of omission and sins of commission, sins of thoughtlessness, accidental sins, provoked sins and deliberate, egregious sins. It was the idea of sin that led good but self-conflicted people to the convent, where, unfortunately, many sins of greed, licentiousness and cruelty were expressed and countenanced. A life of holiness was not always so holy. When Paul wrote that "the wages of sin is death" (Rom. 6:23), he was speaking of the human condition before one became a devotee of Jesus

Christ. Yet, how often do we learn of the egregious (sinful) behavior of "Christians" after they have supposedly committed themselves to Christ? How is their sin reckoned, especially when it has been deliberate and willful?

If there is a punishment for sin (or for a sinful life), it must be in the nature of that life itself. Yet, even that is hard to say for there are many corrupt souls who go to their graves happy with themselves – as well as many "righteous" persons who die in misery and self-disappointment. You will find In the Bible often statements about the rewards of the good life and the "way of the wicked will perish". But, it is not so. Justice does not always prevail. The quality of one's life is its own reward.

Perhaps the idea of sin needs to be cast aside and relegated to the archaic. Perhaps we need to think in a more sophisticated way about sin or to discard it altogether in favor of a new idea about ourselves and our behavior. Maybe we need to categorize our sins and think anew about our condition and our lives.

HEAVEN & HELL

There is no concept of Hell in the Old Testament and only a vague concept of any after-life. At death, one goes down to Sheol, the place of the dead. It is not a place of salvation or of punishment but simply an abode of death. Sheol is used about 80 times in the Old Testament. There is no sense in the Old Testament that one will be rewarded for a good and godly life or punished for a bad one. One simply dies and goes to rest with the fathers. Job looks for justice during his earthly life, not *post mortem*. When the prophets speak of salvation, it is almost always in regard to the nation, with respect to protection against advancing foreign powers who will attack the Kingdoms of Israel and Judah and, later, with regard to the return from Exile.

In fact, the word HELL is not even mentioned in the Old Testament – and New Testament references to it (and they are subject to the Hellenistic influence of the time) are few. In Matthew, there are seven mentions of Hell but Mark only uses the word three times and

Luke and John only use the word once each. In the apostolic letters, it is cited only once in James and once in 2 Peter. Paul never used the word.

Our idea of HELL, as well as that of HEAVEN, is derived from the seventeenth century writer John Milton, who penned *Paradise Lost* and *Paradise Regained*, vivid descriptions of eternities of damnation and salvation that he derived from folklore and wove into vast scenarios of what supposedly were deserved by those he considered the good and the bad. Nothing in the Biblical literature justified the pictures he portrayed.

THE AFTER-LIFE

In the interim between the Old Testament era, around 300 B.C.E., and the Christian era, the Greeks defeated the Persians and occupied Palestine, bringing with it elements of their culture and philosophy. Thus was born among the Jews the idea of an after-life and a rectification of one's life on earth. Even with Jesus of Nazareth, it was not an important idea. But, it was with Paul, a Jewish man schooled in Greek thought, that the idea of salvation in the after-life was promulgated. Eternal life is a not really a Jewish concept but one later adopted from the Greeks.

So, the idea of an after-life is not unique to Christianity. But, it is understandable as to why it arose in many other cultures. In the time prior to the twentieth century, for most people, life was hard and short, regardless of where one lived. Infection was rampant and untreatable; broken bones caused permanent deformities; diseases were scurrilous and often lethal. The average life span was around 40 years. Life was so short and perilous that one could only hope for relief and rectification of misfortune and injustice though an after-life. At least, one could hope. So, religion and the idea of salvation embraced the concept of an after-life or eternal life to give credence to this hope.

Through the ages, Christian thought has heralded this idea of an after-life where God will, in some way, rectify one's life on earth. The wicked will be damned to Hell and the righteous (those who believe Jesus is the Son of God) will be saved and rewarded in Heaven. The idea of rectification is not unique to Christian culture nor is it unexpected. We yearn for injustices and cruelties to be punished and goodness to be rewarded. Apart from that, there is no reason to believe that anything exists beyond the point of physical death and all attempts to define the "eternal soul" are just wishful thinking We live in an age when we understand that human beings are just another stage of evolutionary development in the course of life, another form of animal life. We may be smarter, more creative, more ingenious in what we create than other animals. But, we are still another form of animal life with the same organs and functions as other mammals. One thing that is more highly developed in most of us, however, is our moral sense, an issue we will proceed to discuss later in this discourse.

So, if we dismiss the idea of an "eternal soul", the idea of salvation is moot. There is nothing to be saved from – except ourselves in this life. Consider this also: if our mortal life's purpose is to achieve salvation, isn't that a basically selfish goal? It opposes the idea of selfless sacrifice in living for others or, as Jesus said, "Love one another" and "No man has greater love than this: that he lay down his life for his friend." The only indication that Jesus gave assurance of an after-life is when John quotes him as saying to the other man on the cross: "Today you shall be with me in Paradise" – and that was written sixty to seventy years after the Crucifixion.

If we are realistic, we must conclude that the world is not just. Were it so, Hitler and Stalin and their ilk would suffer far, far greater punishment that the non-believing bully. The compassionate and righteous would receive much greater rewards, both in this life as well as in the world beyond. But, it is not so. One would hope that the good and righteous would live lives that are their own rewards. But, even that is not always true.

The fact is that Justice does not always prevail. We seek to create some semblance of justice through political institutions, but, even then, we make grievous mistakes. How can there ever be justice for the millions of people killed by Adolf Hitler in Europe in the thirties and forties? How can the atrocities of the slave trade ever be undone? How can the misdeeds of Stalin ever be rectified? How can massacres – whether of

American Indians in this country in the 19th century or in Armenia in the early 20th century or during the Crusades in the Balkans - ever be undone and the guilty parties punished? Injustice is the prevalent circumstance and those who live in societies where justice is sought are fortunate. But, even there, the guilty are not always apprehended and the innocent, on occasion, are found guilty and punished. The best we can do is to "seek justice and righteousness", though being aware that it often escapes us.

SALVATION & ETERNAL LIFE

The idea of salvation for a future eternal life arose in days of long ago when life was brutally hard, people were oppressed, and there seemed to be no way out of the misery that surrounded people.

That there would be some way of rectifying injustice and deprivation and oppression led to the idea that there must be an after-life where what awaited was a life of bliss for the weary.

RESURRECTION & REDEMPTION

The idea of Resurrection just doesn't exist in the Hebrew Bible: known to Christians as the Old Testament. It was with the belief in the Resurrection of Jesus that the idea that all Christians would be eventually resurrected came into play. Paul was the principal promoter of that idea and the resurrection of Lazarus and the daughter of the publican were read back into the Gospel narrative of Jesus' ministry. Redemption was, as well, an idea developed by Paul to explain why Jesus had been crucified – on behalf of believers whose sins were forgiven thereby.

PROSPERITY

There are today Preachers who promote the idea of Christian prosperity, as though being a Christian will generate monetary rewards to the faithful believers. It's like saying to God, I'll do something for you (believe) if you do something for me (make me rich). Such a deal! These hucksters do well themselves with the money they glean from those who want to believe in this Gospel of Prosperity. This message is precisely the opposite of what Jesus taught. "Go and sell all that you have and give to the poor and come and follow me" "It is easier for a camel to pass through the eye of a needle than for a rich man to enter the Kingdom of God."

In the Old Testament, the book of Job recounts the experience of a righteous man suffering the pangs of misfortune and wondering why God has punished him. It is an eternal question: why do the wicked prosper and the righteous suffer so horribly? It is a question for which there is no answer – unless it's just that living one's life for others is its own reward.

The best one can say is, comparisons are fraught with danger. You may not be able to change your external circumstances and you can only deal with the way in which you deal with adversity. If there is a lesson to be learned here, it is that the righteous deal better with hardship than the unrighteous because they have a keener regard for themselves as Godly creatures.

JUSTICE

Justice is not defined in the Bible although it is frequently used to indicate fair treatment, forgiveness (at least in cases where the guilty repent) and righteous living. But, Justice is a key concept for the prophets who rail against injustice, where the general populace is treated unfairly, where wrongs go uncorrected, where people are taken advantage of, where poverty is left unattended, where criminal behavior is ignored, where wealth covers up discriminatory behavior.

THE PURPOSE OF LIFE

The quest to define life's purpose has become a kind of joke, as if it is either obvious or hopelessly elusive. For the hedonist, it is the full enjoyment of what life has to offer, whether in an artistic sense or in a basic, sensual form. For the impoverished and dispossessed, it is mere survival for as long as possible. For the competitive, it is winning at every contest.

In the Calvinistic catechism, the purpose of life is to "love God and to enjoy Him forever." It is defined from the outside, ordained by God, universal and applies to everyone. It is an outward view of life. But, in an ultimate sense, there is no difference between individuals. We are all dust – and to dust we shall return.

For the Existentialist, it is whatever you want to identify as the purpose of life, the purpose you give to your life. It is defined by you, within whatever limitations you may have and with whatever abilities you may be able to express.

As far as we know, Jesus never attempted to define "the purpose of life", although he certainly gave clues to what he considered to be the purposeful life. In the parable of the Mustard Seed, he suggested that each person should attempt to grow into the fullest possible expression of his or her personhood. In the Parable of the Good Samaritan, he suggested that we are responsible for one another regardless of who the other person is. If there is one way to characterize how Jesus looked upon each person's role in life, it is that we share responsibility for one another and must live in that way.

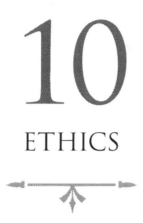

ETHICS

ETHICS – WHAT IT'S IMPORTANT TO KNOW FROM THE BIBLE

Because the Bible is a collection of writings collected from people of many different traditions and perspectives, there is no single ethic that is consistent – except, perhaps, to fear or respect God. But, even God is perceived in different ways. As Elohim (a plural noun), God is perceived as the Creator. As Yahweh, He is the Lawgiver and Judge. As Adonai, He is the Lord and the One to be feared. For the Psalmist, He is the Comforter and the Source of one's blessings (also a mountain dweller – Ps. 121)). For the prophets, He is the One who demands justice and righteousness – for the poor and outcast and even for one's enemies. For the rabbis of Jesus' time, God is all of these, wrapped into One. So, the ethical mandate is ambiguous if one takes the Old Testament as a whole. But, over time, there was a progression in the understanding of Who God is, with the high point being the era of the prophets who sought justice, righteousness and compassion.

As in contemporary times, there were those in Israeli society who attempted to dominate and exploit others of lesser means and stature. The most obvious example of this is the treatment of Uriah, the husband of Bathsheba, by King David. Uriah is killed in order for David to abscond with the wife of Uriah. But, there are other examples of outrageous exploitation of less fortunate people that the prophets condemned.

"Let justice roll down like waters and righteousness like an ever-flowing stream" exclaimed Amos.

We find Jesus most clearly in the prophetic tradition, certainly not in the priestly tradition and clearly not in the royal tradition. There is no sense in which he sought the return of the Jewish monarchy or had much respect for the Temple priests. But, he frequently quotes the prophets such as Isaiah and Jeremiah.

With respect to the Law, he acknowledges the Law of Moses but does not consider himself bound by it – or, at least, by a narrow interpretation of it. So, he approves of his disciples gathering grain from the fields on the Sabbath; he heals on the Sabbath; and he even consoles the woman accused of adultery.

WHAT IT'S IMPORTANT TO KNOW FROM THE CHRISTIAN TRADITION

In its early years, Christianity spread like wildfire to all parts of the known world, east to India and west to Rome and even to Spain, north to the Baltics and south to Ethiopia. The form in which it evolved in these different parts of the world tended to be unique and was formed, in part, by its traditions and environment. Early Gospels and early celebrations represent these differences. The form in which Christianity prevailed was that represented by Istanbul and Rome and, to a lesser extent, by the Coptic churches of Egypt and India.

If the Christian communities of the first century were characterized by tolerance, peace and love, there were eruptions of anger and hatred that showed up in the second century, arguments over the nature and divinity of Jesus and the practice of the church. Eventually, the Christian church that had been persecuted by the dominant society became the persecutor and oppressor of both deviant believers and non-believers.

That intolerance continued from the time of Constantine through the Crusades and the Inquisition up until the modern time. Even today in the United States, there are those who call themselves Christians but seek to oppress non-Christians and atheists.

At the same time, there are those who have chosen the path of peace, tolerance and love. St. Francis of Assisi was one of the earliest of these figures who interpreted the message of Jesus as one of caring for ALL creatures, whether they be more primitive forms of life or human. Albert Schweitzer in the early part of the 20th century followed the same path by living according to his "Reverence for Life" philosophy.

Throughout the centuries, there have been many different ethical expression of the meaning of Christian faith, from the domineering to the obsequious and timid. What we learn from these disparate approaches is that humans tend to make their own systems of ethical response and then use their religious traditions to give them support and credibility. Note that the criminal rationalizes the most heinous acts.

In order to offset this practice (or perhaps to control its constituency), the Church developed the practice of Confession. Unfortunately, by institutionalizing Confession, the practice became rote and meaningless, a way to assuage sins that one could commit and then obtain absolution.

So, Christianity survived for two millennia, not because it carried a message of ethical behavior (which it did) but because it became socially useful. Religion seems to fill that function of providing social cohesion wherever it exists, as it does in all societies for, at least, part of its people. The ethical message seems to be a by-product which is necessary for religion to continue to play a role, even if that message is honored in the breach. People are controlled more by their passions than by any ethical suasion. And yet, there are people who act ethically and even altruistically, who are willing to sacrifice themselves for others.

THE ROLE OF CHRISTIANS TODAY IN THE CONTEMPORARY WORLD

If we are to be followers of Jesus, our purpose in the world is to respect and love our neighbor, even our enemies, to help those in need, to go the extra mile in providing assistance to those who need it. It is not easy. The needs are innumerable and sometimes beyond our capacity to meet what is demanded. There are those who would take advantage of our generosity and even those who would do us harm. Nonetheless, Jesus asks us to take some risks and to do our best.

The world has become much more complex than it was in Jesus' day. Populations have increased, the ability to travel far greater distances has exploded, technology has become very sophisticated, business activities are more complex, medical technology allows us to live much longer, communications are far more extensive, and human interactions have intensified. People are better educated, information is infinitely greater and immediately accessible, and national and community laws are far more intricate. Needless to say, whereas human impacts upon the environment were once negligible, they are now significant and threaten the survival of most forms of multicellular life on this planet.

Two thousand years ago, when Rome ruled the known world, the ability of governments to make a positive impact upon the world was quite limited. What governments did for the people was to provide a unified defense against outside marauders and to provide a stable framework for the city marketplace. Governments did little to provide social services for the weak and disenfranchised.

Today, government is, in varying degrees, regarded as the source of relief for society's ills, whether it be merely tariffs to protect indigenous business interests or to be the provider of medical aid and retirement security. Curing social problems is now seen as a government responsibility. Still, there are ongoing arguments about **whether** that should be the role of government as well as **how** will be the most effective way to solve the issue at hand.

The issues today are so huge and complex that easy answers are not obvious. So, what role does the follower of Jesus play in this tableau?

One thing is clear: that the Christian is bound to confront social problems and to find any effective way that they might be resolved as quickly as possible. The lives of people are involved, and their welfare is at stake. So, let's enumerate the primary issues that Christians are properly concerned about as ethical issues:

Food for the Poor	Teenage Pregnancy	Discrimination – Racial, Ethnic, Religious, etc.
Shelter for the Poor	Runaway children	Human Rights
Family planning	Suicide	Civil Rights
Pregnancy care	Criminal behavior & Rehabilitation	
	False Accusations & Perjured Testimony	
Natology (Birthing)	Use & Abuse of Drugs	
Infant care and child care	Alcoholism	Senior mobility
Medical care for children	Smoking addiction	Senior abuse
Child abuse and forced child labor	Gambling Addiction	Poverty
Sexual predation on children	Rape & Physical Abuse	Animal Abuse
Childhood education	Spousal Abuse	
Special Needs of the Disabled & handicapped		
	Incarceration & Detention	

Organizations exist to respond to each and every one of these social problems. So, apart from what you can do individually to help others who are victims of these problems, you can make yourself available through an organization to help others who could use your help.

What it Means to be a Christian Today – Going Beyond the Ordinary: Volunteerism

As I have noted above, Jesus was a teacher of ethics – even if he didn't call his teaching by that name. He abhorred hypocrisy and false religion and encouraged true compassion for other human beings. Take the Parable of the Good Samaritan, the man who had been beaten and bypassed on the road by a couple of Jews, one of whom was a rabbi. It was a Samaritan, someone who was despised and rejected by the Jews, someone you would not have expected to show compassion on a fallen Jew, who came to the man's rescue and nursed him back to health. It's a Parable, not a true story as far as we know. But, it illustrates what it was that Jesus expects of human beings. It's a study in the ethical responsibility we have for everyone, regardless of who we are.

Of course, ethical decisions are not all as easy as with the Good Samaritan Parable. There are difficult choices with which we are confronted and the most ethical choice is not always apparent.

EMPATHY

People who love their pets empathize with their needs. You understand when they need to go out to relieve themselves and when they want to eat. If they injure themselves in some way, you attempt to relieve their suffering, if only by cuddling them and trying to soothe their pain. People who care about their pets identify with their needs and do their best to respond. It's called empathy.

But, it's only a pet, a dumb animal. It's not your child. Your pet isn't human. It's only a pet. Why should you care? Why should you sense your pet's discomfort and feel that need to respond to it? But, maybe you don't. Not all people identify and empathize with their pets as much as others. People differ that way in how they respond. We empathize in different ways and we respond differently to various animals and people. Nonetheless, we see in some narcisstic political figures a blatant disregard for the welfare of others whom they choose to neglect – or even harm – by the policies they advocate and the actions they take.

Even so, people tend to be selective in where they show empathy – as when one cares for one's own pet but is oblivious to the needs of other animals - as when someone cherishes one's own family members but seeks to do harm to others. Some people are more empathetic than others. Some people become more insensitive to others – less empathetic than others. Nonetheless, empathy is a character trait most people experience, though more intense for some than for others. It is a characteristic of the Christian and a trait encouraged by Jesus:

"What you have done to one of the least of these, my brethren, you have done to me." "Love your neighbor as yourself." Empathy is the ethic of the Christian.

Empathy is a projection of yourself into the being of another – to understand how the other feels – and thinks – and needs. Empathy is an identification with the other so that you feel what the other feels – and care about it. Empathy is the motivation for action on behalf of the other.

Empathy can be universal, meaning it can apply to all things. While ethical discourse is primarily directed toward other people, it can be directed to other living creatures, even to inanimate objects. We can empathize not only with pets but with other animals, including farm animals and wildlife. It can be a constraint against hunting and trapping, even against butchering. Those who write stories about trees and plants and portray them in conversation have projected an empathetic identity onto them.

Each of us must understand - decide - the limit of our empathy. But, some of us have a very narrow limit to our empathy, having little care or concern for the feelings of others. We generally consider those people to be psychopathic or sociopathic and divorced from the normal range of human feelings. They can probably not be redeemed and are eventually incarcerated to keep them from harming others beyond what they have already done.

The Christian ethic would have us maximize our empathy – and learn to live not so much for ourselves but for the good and benefit of others. How we do that is what Jesus encouraged his followers to do – and what he himself exhibited in his life and death. It is why his followers celebrated his resurrection.

How Churches Need to Adjust

Churches perform some important functions in society. They bring people together and provide a community for dialogue. They identify needy people and needed services within their communities and develop helpful responses. They provide a meeting place for groups such as AA, NAACP, Scouts, Audubon and Habitat for Humanity, activities that actually perform services for people. They provide a place for communal worship and meditation that allows people to reflect on their lives and restore their mental health.

Churches need to be centers for discussion about critical ethical issues. They need to foment discussion instead of their more common role of stifling discussion about important issues. Controversy should not be alien to the church environment. What churches need to do is to become more involved in issues that are more significant to the social fabric and that are more focused on social justice: Labor issues, peace, criminal justice, poverty, the environment, racial justice, economic justice, etc. - these are the issues that should be discussed within the churches because they deal primarily with social ethics – the principal focus of Jesus during his ministry. They should be active in doing what they can to create a society that is more dedicated to achieving justice and support for everyone.

No doubt, that is a major adjustment from the current focus of most churches. There will undoubtedly be some resistance, even defections, as we have seen over the ordination of women, ending capital punishment, family planning, the welcoming of homosexuals and the acceptance of same-sex marriage. People will have different viewpoints on issues – but the objective is to encourage people to consider each issue from an ethical, Christian perspective, to listen carefully to one another, to respect varying viewpoints, to work together to find acceptable answers, and to be involved in activities that will implement those answers.

LIVING RESPONSIBLE AND MEANINGFUL LIVES

A few years ago, Rick Warren published *A Purpose Driven Life*, its title indicating for Christians the real meaning of the faith, not only for one's good mental health but also one's responsibility to the community in which one lives. In order to be truly healthy, one needs purpose and goals outside of oneself, making a positive contribution to the community. Regardless of where one is positioned in life, one needs to have an objective that makes life better for others. Focusing just on oneself, though that is important, is not enough. Giving outwardly of oneself is what is just as important and makes life worth living.

CHRISTIAN ETHICS

Jesus encouraged his followers to follow an ethic of understanding and compassion, to be focused on decisions that were thoughtful, humane and intelligent – to show empathy in dealing with others. He lived in a different time when public issues were much simpler to resolve than we find posed to us today. Health care, nuclear war, public education, abortion, toxicity, immigration and gun issues did not exist as prominent issues two thousand years ago.

To confront, consider and position ourselves on these issues from the point of view of Christian responsibility, we need to extrapolate from what Jesus taught. That, in itself, is not easy. It relies on thought and consideration of what Jesus taught and thought. It relies on reason and a consideration of the facts as we have discovered and uncovered them. In the end, our ethical judgments must be informed by a communal understanding of what is determined to be the most responsible judgment and conclusion. In the end, our judgments must not be absolute or dogmatic, but rather flexible, tentative and tolerant. They must be open to new information and understanding and not reek of superiority. Above all, they must be characterized by compassion toward others, particularly those without power or wealth.

When Jesus was asked which was the greatest commandment, he responded with this comment that actually summarizes the basis of all Christian ethics: "You shall love your God with all your heart, with all your soul, and with all your mind. And, you shall love your neighbor as yourself." It might be reworded as "You owe a higher ethical loyalty in your life that is outside yourself. You need to love others as much as you love yourself."

I have always been bothered by religionists who have emphasized salvation of one's own soul, which seemed like a perfectly selfish endeavor while Jesus bids us to make our lives meaningful by living for the benefit and welfare of others. Don't demean yourself but respect others at least as much as you respect yourself. With that as the starting point, other ethical prescriptions can be drawn.

11

EXPRESSIONS OF CHRISTIANITY

CHRISTIANS OVER THE AGES

Without Paul (Saul of Tarsus) and his evangelizing efforts in the eastern Mediterranean, Christianity almost surely would have died out. There is no evidence that Jesus of Nazareth ever intended to found (i.e. establish) a church. He believed the End was near and he prepared his disciples to be ready for it. What we know as Christianity today is largely the work of Paul and his interpretation of who Jesus was. Albert Schweitzer, in his book *The Mysticism of Paul the Apostle*, argues that it was Paul who imbued Jesus with divinity and envisioned a spiritual unity of the believer with the Messiah. While the Gospel writers, who wrote after Paul, also quote some remarks from Jesus about his divinity, it was Paul who initiated the argument. Much of Christian theology emanates from Paul, not Jesus.

The early church was comprised of people who regarded Jesus as their Lord. "Jesus is Lord" was the early confession of faith. No theological statements of the nature of Christ, no Trinitarian compositions, no assertions of Godly unity. Just a commitment to follow the teachings of Jesus. There were no church buildings, no ecclesiastical hierarchy, no governing councils. People met in homes to sing and talk with one another about the meaning of Jesus for their lives. There were no Gospels to be read, only letters from Paul and others to discuss and think about. They understood that their mission was to help others and to show their compassion. But, gradually, a leadership developed and then a hierarchy and eventually meeting places were established – and then great cathedrals. The original purpose and mission was given less importance and the trappings of an authoritarian hierarchical institution took over.

Initially, the assemblies of Christians were passive and pacifistic as regards the imperial authority of Rome. Not until the time of Constantine in the fourth century did Christians adopt more militaristic characteristics. However, even in the second century, there were violent arguments over matters of doctrine and even some killings. The internal arguments among Christians were remarkably hostile and vitriolic, arguing over the humanity or divinity of Jesus and eventually settling on both. Docetists argued that Jesus had no corporeal form whereas others argued that he was only a prophet. Gnostics taught that Jesus imparted secret knowledge and that becoming a Christian involved an initiation into that knowledge. Even defining the Canon of the New Testament resulted in bitter arguments and angry fights over what we would today consider irrelevancies.

The Crusades of the tenth to the twelfth centuries, carried out in the name of Jesus, were terrible adventures resulting in much brutality, death and destruction. Even Crusading forces fought among themselves. Considering that Jesus asked us to love our enemies and treated people with affection and dignity, how can it be that his followers can act this way – and use his name to justify their actions? Yet, in our own time, we have "Christian militias" and warriors who claim to fight in the name of Jesus. We have enclaves of Christians who feel besieged and want to fight to destroy others and defend, in militant fashion, the "Christian way of life". There are those who call the United States a "Christian nation" and regard the nation as superior because it is "Christian". That's hardly what Jesus had in mind.

THE REFORMATION

During the Middle Ages, the Catholic church dominated European culture as the overarching authority. Prudence dictated keeping quiet instead of expressing disagreement, whether about the authority of the church or about doctrine (as with Galileo). Those who challenged the church, either paid for it with imprisonment or worse OR only did so from a position of alternative power. Civil rights were unknown in practice and blasphemous in theory. In the fourteenth and fifteenth centuries, the authority of the church began to weaken because of internal corruption. Certain dissident voices were heard, demanding access to the Bible, challenging certain theological doctrines and questioning some religious practices. A few reformers paid with their lives.

In 1517, Martin Luther is credited with posting his Ninety-Five Theses to the door of the Wittenberg church, regarded as the beginning of the Protestant Reformation. The significance of this was the beginning of a dialog about the underlying theology of the church, questioning the practice of the sale of indulgences (for the forgiveness of sin), and proposing that salvation was by faith and not solely the purview of the church. In a societal sense, this undermined the role and place of the Roman Catholic church in the culture of Europe. In protesting the sale of Indulgences by the Roman Church, Luther was suggesting that Rome was improperly representing the Christian faith. Luther's protest was by no means the first effort to challenge Rome, but it was the first to successfully do so with a major impact on the society of the Middle Ages. Whether it was because of the time or the circumstances of the day, Luther's challenge was subsequently joined by John Calvin in Switzerland, Zwingli in Germany and a host of other more liberated thinkers and churchmen who took issue in various ways with the theology and practices of the church. These dissident events were then seized upon by princes and political leaders to support their grievances with Rome's domination of their political fiefdoms, commencing in the dissolution of European hegemony.

The Reformers were not speaking to the political situation directly, though they were aided in their separation from the church by the political forces that were thereby released. The implications of the Gospel for the social and political situation of the day were not readily apparent. State churches remained in most places, closely aligned with the princes, and further dissention was tolerated only in varying degrees – and at varying times. In England, with the separation of the Anglican church from Rome by Henry VIII, there remained a church hierarchy and bureaucracy and a religious conformity, from which religious dissidents were from time to time oppressed.

THE PURITAN EXPERIMENT

Early in the 17th century, a group of dissidents had formed in England, known as the Puritans because they were disillusioned by corruption in the Anglican Church and wanted to "purify" it. While they were not separatists from the church, they were regarded as bothersome renegades by the clergy and king and were periodically persecuted. In response, some fled to Holland and elsewhere – and then sought refuge in the new land of America. However, they too were a cohesive group who bore no tolerance of dissidents and developed an increasingly hostile relationship with their Native American hosts.

As more Europeans arrived on American shores, they brought with them contagious diseases which decimated the native Indian villages nearby, enabling the Europeans to secure more land for farming and establish their own villages. If there was a purpose in befriending the Indians, it was not to share culture for their benefit but to Christianize and dominate them. The 18th and 19th centuries were to continue this approach.

THE SOCIAL GOSPEL

Religion in early America was predominantly structured around church attendance on Sundays and, to a lesser extent, with a midweek service. Churchgoing became an indicator of a stabilized community and of a parishioner's acceptable position in the community. To be recognized as "a good citizen", it was important to belong to a church. Among Protestant churches, Episcopalian, Presbyterian, Lutheran and Congregationalist provided the greatest prestige while Methodist was more the "workingman's" church. Baptists and Pentecostals carried even less prestige. Frontier America became the vineyard for the Methodists and Baptists. These early expressions of religion were largely social conventions, providing a socializing opportunity for congregants and devising various conventions to meet their economic needs. Any interest in social reform or political concern for the unchurched poor was largely absent – with the exception of slavery.

Abolition took hold in many of the churches in the North while the churches in the South became its defenders, causing many denominations to divide, ruptures that lasted until the latter part of the 20th century when, in the era of the Civil Rights movement, church leaders saw the folly and shame of their separation.

Attitudes toward social reform began to change, at least in some churches, primarily in the North, with the popularity of the works of Charles Dickens in the middle of the 19th century and with the burgeoning labor movement in the period following the Civil war, when attitudes toward the social and economic power of the newly dominant corporations started to shift. The plight of the poor and dispossessed slowly crept into America's conscience with the nature of the economic system being targeted for blame. The class divide became more pronounced.

Beginning in the 1890s, several pastors who worked in or near the city slums began to promote the idea that the social and political order needed to change on behalf of the disenfranchised and the poor – and that the churches had a responsibility to lead the way. This movement, largely led by pastors including Walter Rauschenbush, Washington Gladden, Harry Emerson Fosdick and others was named the "Social Gospel" and captivated many in the more "liberal" churches. Ronald Osborne has written:

"The liberal movement in theology embraced the social gospel, but did not acquire a monopoly on its preaching. Especially during the Great Depression beginning in 1929, when the minds of laymen were troubled by questions concerning our economic system, many sermons sounded from our pulpits dealing with international relations, unemployment, race relations, and other current problems. The time was hopeful, if men would turn to the way of Jesus, a better day was at hand."

The Social Gospel looked forward to the arrival of the Kingdom of God in America, the proponents naively believed that their efforts to Christianize the people of America would inaugurate a time and place where poverty, want and injustice, would disappear and an egalitarian community would emerge and prevail.

FUNDAMENTALISTS AND EVANGELICALS

It is a grievous experience to encounter those who claim to be the followers of Jesus, yet in word and practice are speaking and acting in precisely the manner that he was trying to countermand. Mindless and irrelevant doctrine in place of compassion and common sense and truth are anathema to what we should understand Jesus was trying to achieve. Evangelicals would have us believe that Jesus is the only way to salvation and a fulfilling life, that only by saying the right phrases will one achieve a heavenly reward, that only by "accepting Christ as one's Lord and Savior" is one verifiably a Christian and able to hope for eternal life. They want converts to become one with Christ and to be "saved".

What is difficult to understand is how those who have done so – notably many of the evangelical preachers – can become embroiled in the financial and sexual scandals that have emerged to the light of day. If they are unified with Christ and saved, how can it be that they have succumbed to temptation and wandered so far?

UNITARIANS AND UNIVERSALISTS

Universalists and Unitarians grew out of the Congregational Church in New England in the late 1700s where they simply could not abide the Trinitarian theology of the traditional church but still considered themselves Christians in a less dogmatic style. Over time, however, Unitarians have become tolerant and inclusive of anyone who embraces a "spiritual" approach to life, even if that means no belief in God. Unitarian-Universalists, who got together and merged their denominations in 1961, tend to be "liberal" politically and activist in social and political causes.

WHAT IT MEANS TO BE CHRISTIAN TODAY

In the United States today, there is a wide spectrum to the meaning of being identified as "Christian", generally running the gamut of being militantly religious (even allowing for violence against those perceived as one's enemies) to those who interpret the Bible in a very liberal fashion, hold to a very progressive theology and embrace extremely humanistic causes. If one is identified as a Christian in American society, however, the general assumption is that one embraces a fairly centrist or even conservative religious (theological) perspective and a corresponding politics. BUT, that is not necessarily the case.

The word "Christian" is an ambiguous term although the context of its usage helps to clarify what is meant. In its basic form, "Christian" identifies the religious commitment of a person, the belief in Jesus Christ as divine and the Savior or Redeemer of the world. In Paul's meaning of the word, it meant that one was mystically joined to Christ and represented Christ in the contemporary world.

As the Christian church grew, the word "Christian" identified one as a member or participant in the church and less as one deeply involved spiritually or religiously committed. That meaning was succeeded by its interpretation as a member of a civil community that had an historic relationship to the Christian church. So, one could be identified as

"Christian" just by living in a town or community that was dominated by a strand of the Christian church. In other words, Christians tended to live together, even though they might not be involved in the activities or rituals of the church or hold to orthodox Christian beliefs. This is the more common understanding of the term today, that of an ethnic identity, in essence, a tribal group. So, when a community in the Middle East is attacked by terrorists today, it really identifies its history or dominant religion rather than its important religious practice or commitment.

As we use the term "Christian" in America today, it usually means that one is a member of a church that identifies itself as Christian. While it can be assumed that one holds certain beliefs because of one's church identity, it is not necessarily so. If those in the pews were questioned about their true beliefs, it is likely that there would be considerable deviation from the church's orthodoxy.

Arguments today over the issue of whether the United States is "a Christian nation", even in the most rigorous sense, have to do with the country's founding and whether the Founders were Christian in their identity or intent in writing the Constitution. Most historians agree that Franklin, Jefferson, Madison, and Monroe, even Washington, were deists in their personal beliefs. Jefferson even published a New Testament in which the miracles were deleted from the Gospels since he didn't believe in their historical accuracy. The argument has to do with whether religion, usually in the form of Christianity, deserves certain rights and privileges from government, privileges that can be enforced.

But, if we ask the question in a different way and inquire about the traits of the Christian character, one would have to come up with terms such as humble, loving, compassionate, merciful, reverential, just, generous, kind, honest and truthful. The Christian is dedicated to righteousness, committed to fairness, characterized as forgiving, passionate for justice, and willing to sacrifice oneself for others. The Christian extends himself/herself to be kind and helpful to others, to seek out ways to make the lives of others more fruitful and meaningful.

12

CONTEMPORARY ISSUES OF IMPORTANCE TODAY

CRITICAL CONTEMPORARY ISSUES

The world today is a far more complex environment than was the world of Jesus' day. Many of the ethical problems with which we are currently confronted just didn't exist 2000 years ago. Technology has posed issues, such as cloning and stem cell research, that just didn't exist even a few years ago. As these issues develop and confront us, there are disputes that arise, as there should be – for these developments pose new and serious issues. So, we have to consider these problems and issues in the context of Jesus' teachings. There are no hard and fast answers. At the same time, people who consider these issues should not be condemned for the conclusions they reach - for the ethical response is in the recognition that it is **the process of evaluation**, not necessarily in the conclusions, that is important. It would be tempting, for example, to condemn the gun culture in America because of the many deaths that are attributed to it. But, perhaps a case can be made for allowing gun ownership in order to protect oneself as well as others in violent situations – and to cull certain overpopulations of wildlife where starvation might otherwise occur. Still, one should be aware of the dangers of gun use & carry - and proper restrictions should be willingly implemented and observed.

The point is that Jesus did not address most of the ethical decisions that we must face today – so there can be no specific guidance for how we should respond. He did, however, provide the general guidelines for ethical decision-making – and rely on our own thinking for an appropriate response. That leaves room for debate since ethical decisions are usually complex and answers not always obvious. Dialogue is often helpful in discovering other aspects to the debate that haven't previously occurred to those who are trying to find ethically sustainable answers. Except in the more extreme situations (e.g. slavery), there are seldom absolutely clear answers.

A Christian Ideal for Society

When we consider Jesus' *modus operandi*, several things are clear:

1. He was a humanitarian, respecting the humanity and dignity of those he encountered (or calling them to it), showing compassion for those who were troubled, trodden down or poor, healing the sick, nurturing the beleaguered, restoring the outcast.
2. He rejected intolerance of any kind, based on national/cultural origin, race, gender or religion.
3. He despised hypocrisy and false religiosity.
4. He asked those he met to consider their values – and rejected the false values of pride, political position and wealth.
5. He called people to consider their intrinsic worth and see themselves as worthy and deserving respect.
6. He valued truth.

The Role of the Christian Today in the Contemporary World

UNIVERSAL ISSUES

Human Rights & Civil Rights

In a civilized world, we acknowledge the right of every person to certain **human rights**: the right to live out our lives without attack or interference by others, the right to be free of pain or torture inflicted by others (freedom from fear), the right to care and comfort when injured or afflicted, the right to own personal property, the right to move about freely in public space (i.e. to travel), the right to think freely and to express our thoughts (free speech), the right to privacy, and the right to worship as one pleases without coercion or interference. These are basic human rights that should be enjoyed by everyone, though they are not. These rights are not endowed by heavenly mandate but they are not transient. We assert that they are universally valid. They cannot be applied discriminately but are inherent in our being. No one would want to dispense with any of these rights for himself/herself and, for that reason, they belong to everyone – except for those who would deprive them of others. Human Rights are based on the principle of the Integrity of the individual in a Humane World.

Human rights are distinct from **civil rights** which are created and established by law. Civil rights, however, are derived from human rights. The right to vote is a civil right within a political system. The right to own property, the right to file a lawsuit and the right to drive a vehicle are rights established by law. They can be restricted by law but they cannot be applied in a discriminatory fashion. Civil rights are based upon the principles of Fairness and Equality in a civil society.

The basic responsibility of government is to respect the **human rights** of everyone, whether citizen or not. Jesus made no distinctions, and neither should we. All people should be regarded as equal in the sight of God. The recognition of basic human rights was codified in the U.N.'s Universal Declaration of Human Rights and supports the establishment of civil rights and its codification in structures of government around the globe. The recognition of civil rights was embodied in the U.S. Bill of Rights (first ten Amendments to the

U.S. Constitution). Basic civil rights are now recognized by many governments throughout the world. Unfortunately, there are too many countries who still ignore the Universal Declaration of Human Rights and act in violation of the Declaration.

The Christian ethic values a world of order among people. Respect for Human Rights and Civil Rights are inherent in the Christian ethic. Otherwise, injustice, chaos and cruelty prevail, without personal security for anyone. The Christian ethic of Fairness and Respect for Human Life and Integrity are mandated by our humanity to prevail.

THE UNIVERSAL DECLARATION of Human Rights

UNITED NATIONS

Democracy Everywhere

Democracy, the will and power of the people, is not new. It was intermittently practiced by the ancient Greeks and Romans. But, it was always lurking in the background as the most just and desirable overarching form of government, representing the best expression of the right of humans to be human and the responsibility of government to recognize the civil right of every person to free expression without censure. In the modern world, democratic forms of government are universally recognized as the best way to organize a government. Though not perfect in their expression, democratic forms of government were largely inspired by Christian ethics. (There is an argument that American democracy was, in part, inspired by the Iroquois confederacy.) Democracies represent the best form of celebrating human rights and the basic civil rights of the people. As Winston Churchill famously noted, "It has been said that democracy is the worst form of government except for all the others that have been tried."

Laws Just and Spurious

Laws and ethics are independent of each other, though they are often confused. Laws usually arise from an ethical foundation, though not always. Nor does an ethical judgment always conform to the law – for there are laws placed on the books that are actually unrelated to ethics and even in violation of an ethical perspective. For example, the Pennsylvania Blue Laws, prohibiting the sale of alcohol on Sundays, were laws based on social convention that actually restricted people's behavior for no good reason other than to impose a social control.

Laws that restrict the smoking of tobacco products are justified as ethical because smoking can affect the health of others in enclosed places. A law that requires the wearing of a protective head helmet can be justified, not only to minimize the risk of brain damage in a cycle accident, but also to reduce the exposure and liability of ambulance personnel and others in rescuing and transporting the injured cyclist.

Spurious laws help no one and are simply written as a means of controlling the behavior of others or to satisfy the biases of their authors for a privately held social norm or to impose a control on an out-of-favor group of people. Christian ethics can hardly be used to justify such laws. The Civil Rights movement based its efforts on the premise that it needed to flout the laws on the books because they were immoral laws that needed to be challenged in a non-violent way. Other laws may be regarded as immoral when they discriminate against certain groups of people.

So, laws can be used in such a way as to discriminate and even punish people in an unjustifiable manner. Thus, in many places in the South in the first half of the 20th century, laws existed to keep African-Americans out of certain places (such as restaurants), even public places (swimming pools, rest rooms, etc.). They required blacks to sit in the back of the bus or movie theatre. They prohibited interracial marriage (not limited to the South). Laws discriminated in many ways – and continue to do so today.

For the prophets of the Old Testament, justice was a supremely important value – and they continually saw instances of injustice and the negligence of authorities to rectify it, let alone to stop perpetrating it.

THE ROLE & NATURE OF GOVERNMENT IN A DEMOCRATIC SOCIETY

The Christian brings his/her ethical code to the governmental/political arena. With democratic political systems, it is much easier, though less challenging, to do so. In an environment where one can speak freely and provide support for the disharmonious and disenfranchised, even the criminal, without repercussions, it is less dangerous, less socially objectionable, and more tolerable to do so. Christians in a hostile environment (e.g. totalitarian regimes) are more concerned with the safety, mutual responsibility and the welfare of other people and their own community than with the mode of government. There wasn't much Christians could do about the actions of the Roman Senate or the Emperor. Totalitarian regimes exist today in which Christians are repressed, if not persecuted, despite their commitment to help others.

In modern democratic societies, the Christian can be more focused on the attitude and position of the state – and concerned with issues of justice, the responsibilities of government and the rights of various peoples subject to governance. So, the people can force government to be more responsive and servicing to the people, as long as the people pay attention. The Christian can play a role in encouraging people to be more caring for one another, more honest and responsible and informed. Encouraging good citizenship is an important task of the Christian.

The objective of government is to serve its people. So, to do this, government needs to set the example for honesty, responsibility and respect. There is no place in government for bribery, corruption, falsehoods, or discrimination. Government needs to be fair and just, transparent and honest. Christians need to see that government fulfills its proper role.

TAXES

Taxes have always been controversial. Even to the point of questioning whether the state has the right to impose taxes on its citizens. There is probably no place on earth where one can go to escape some kind of tax. Some people have questioned whether the state has the right to tax the income one has generated through his/her hard work. Tax collectors have been despised down through the ages. At times, in history, tax collectors have been entitled to keep for their own use a portion of the money they collected from others. Taxes have been used by authoritarian regimes to suppress citizens and to enrich the authorities. There is no doubt that there are many instances where taxes have been abusive and used by the authorities for their own benefit.

Nonetheless, taxes have universally been deemed necessary to provide essential benefits for people in society, benefits that are frequently glossed over and not recognized, even by those who benefit from them. Most governments, at their inception, are charged by the people they serve to collect and spend tax money for the common good. When the U.S. was founded, tax money was collected to build roads, jails, and schools, plus some persons to care for these activities – and that was about it. With time, the complexity and responsibilities of government grew – as did the population and the demands it placed on government – thereby increasing the need for tax revenue. The sources and complexity of the tax system grew – but so did the benefits people receive from paying taxes.

Unfortunately, a few public figures are wasteful, irresponsible, even larcenous, with tax money – and give taxes a bad name with the general public. That does not mean taxes are bad. It means the public needs to be better informed and attentive to the ways in which their tax money is used. People benefit greatly when taxes ae used responsibly and effectively.

We have constantly heard the cry: "No more taxes" and the promise of politicians to reduce taxes. But, taxes are an ethical issue that Christians need to see as their obligation to understand, critique and, where important, support. Wasteful spending is clearly a misuse of tax revenue – but reducing taxes with the consequent reduction of important services to people is not responsible citizenship. Responsible citizenship lies within the purview of Christian ethics. It's a responsibility we all need to take seriously and it requires reasonable and fair tax policy, prioritizing expenditures, careful budgeting, honest spending and evaluation of results.

WAR & MILITARY CONFLAGRATIONS

The forces that go into war-making are so enormous that any position the church might take is almost irrelevant. As Nazi Panzers moved across Europe in the late thirties and murdered thousands in their path, the only course of action people could take was either to flee or try to defend themselves in whatever way possible. Even when Iraq invaded Kuwait in 1990, there wasn't much that could be done in any persuasive way. Either accept the status quo & stay out of the way, accept some risk by trying to help victims or find a way to move aggressively against the invader.

If anything is to be done to prevent war (and the killing that goes along with it), it would take an enormous effort on the part of the church –and church people – to create an atmosphere in which war is regarded as unacceptable to any potential aggressor. In the case of the Nazi onslaught against Eastern Europe and then Britain and France, the German people (and a good part of the irrelevant church) felt that a horrendous wrong was being corrected – until it proved too late and the horrors of Nazism became evident.

And, what if you go to war to help your sister nation defend herself – as in Kuwait– or to help the oppressed to free themselves – as in Libya? And what if you make a mistake – as in Vietnam? Is the church just irrelevant when it comes to war? Such issues require lively debate within the church community.

THE ENVIRONMENT

Only recently, has the Environment emerged as an important ethical issue but, even so, only in the eyes of some. There is a tendency to ignore the realities of environmental damage, both now and in the years to come. Heretofore, environmental issues have been largely confined to the realm of the aesthetic. Now, they are beginning to impinge into the economic realm and are receiving more attention because of crop displacement, air and water pollution and other impacts. Rising sea levels due to global warming are only now beginning to flood coastal areas and force people out of their homes but portend severe consequences in the future.

Since environmental changes impact the health of the planet and the lives of so many people, they deserve consideration in the context of ethics, not just as an economic issue (although they will entail tremendous public and private costs). Up until the end of the 18th century, the human impact on the planet was negligible. With the beginning of industrialization in the late 1700s, human-caused factory smoke was introduced into the atmosphere. Its production was accelerated throughout the 19th and 20th centuries, with toxicity steadily increasing because of the increase in the type and number of sources generating pollutants, resulting in a souring of air quality. Similarly, water was affected as pollutants were dumped into rivers and streams without consideration of their impacts. Should we not, then, conclude that air and water are essential sources of life and that they should not be defiled?

Preserving a clean environment is an ethical issue precisely because the environment is the home of all humanity and demands being kept free of contaminants that cause disease and uninhabitable conditions. Those who follow Jesus have a major responsibility not only of keeping the environment clean but of leading the movement to accomplish that purpose.

Technology over the last 250 years has created the need for decisions that just didn't exist in earlier years – and the pace of technology and the complex ethical issues surrounding technological development are huge and difficult. Environmental issues are profoundly greater than earlier inasmuch as the consequences of those decisions are much longer lasting than when it was simply a biodegradable world. It was never before thought that the world had limits of sustainability and that human impacts could be devastating and long lasting.

But, from an ethical perspective, humans have been regarded as stewards of the world and responsible for its maintenance. The Garden of Eden story in Genesis emphasizes that point.

THE RIGHTS OF NATURE

Is Christian ethics essentially anthropocentric – focusing ethical decisions on what is best for humans – or does it extend to other forms of life, and even on to the world itself: rocks, plants, trees, waterways, etc.? Does the world (i.e. Creation) have its own intrinsic value which that it would be best to leave undisturbed? It is a huge question that has multiple advocates on all sides – and should be a germane topic for religious discussion.

GLOBAL WARMING

It is not a question in serious dispute about the rapid warming of the climate over the past century, evidenced by the melting of the polar ice caps, the changing weather and the statistical record. The evidence for the human impact on the atmosphere is indicated by the rapid increase of CO_2 and methane over the past century. So, the question of global warming caused by human activity, supported by an army of scientists, is hardly in doubt. The real question is what, if anything, is to be done about it. It's an ethical question that's important for the Christian community to address, informed by scientific findings, as difficult as they are to prescribe. It's not an irrelevant issue for the concerned Christian, since the lives of everyone are at stake. Everyone should be involved in the discussion and the debate.

Every person on the face of the earth leaves a carbon footprint. Each of us impacts the environment by contributing to the CO2 overload. Each has a responsibility for minimizing his/her contribution to the impact. An important topic for discussion in the church is: What can I, as an individual, do to minimize my carbon imprint and reduce my contribution to global warming.

NUCLEAR POWER

The discovery of nuclear fission opened up the opportunity for the generation of energy without the consumption of fossil fuels, an environmentally favorable development. Nuclear power plants have been constructed but there have been problems. The Chernobyl reactor overheated and spewed radioactive material across the Ukrainian landscape for miles around, resulting in the evacuation of residents in the vicinity. The Diablo Canyon reactor (San Obispo County, California) was built on an earthquake fault and eventually dismantled and abandoned. The Fukushima disaster in Japan, caused by a tsunami, also resulted in the destruction and evacuation of a huge coastal area. The disposal of spent fuel rods, that remain radioactive for thousands of years, is a problem that has not yet been resolved. And yet, were these problems to be solved, nuclear power is an otherwise clean, efficient, and economical way to generate the power needed for a heavily populated world. Its proponents claim that it will solve our need for energy in an environmentally acceptable way.

It's a question that Christian ethicists can and will debate for decades to come – if not longer: how best to serve human needs without causing harm to present and future generations.

POLLUTION

In Jesus' time, pollution was probably not a serious problem and certainly not one that caused much comment or controversy. Most garbage was biodegradable and degraded away. Towns and villages had garbage disposal dumps that kept garbage away from homes and dwellings. Sewage gutters were probably the most significant problem and could have been the source of diseases such as cholera – but the relationship of sewage to disease was not understood. Sewage was likely controlled due to the smell. As a result, pollution was not considered the important issue that it is currently.

What makes pollution a controversial issue today is its relationship to the economy and jobs. There is a cost to controlling the pollution that affects ground water and the air that we breathe. It can translate into a company's profitability as well as to the jobs that can be affected. The control of emissions into the atmosphere costs money. Prevent a chemical plant or a coal company from dumping tailings into a stream – and it costs money to devise an alternative disposal process. Require a pipeline being built to circumvent an environmentally important waterway and it becomes more expensive. Prevent an environmentally destructive factory from being built and it costs jobs. So, what is more important: money, jobs or the environment? From an ethical point of view, what is the answer?

When President Obama issued air pollution regulations for coal-fired power plants that would cost companies substantial amounts of money to rectify, there were howls of protest, claiming the regulations were costly and would be ineffective. Subsequently, President Trump lifted many of these regulations, resulting in further air pollution. Is there an issue of ethics here that Christians should take seriously? No doubt, issues such as this are complex and require some detailed knowledge that most people don't have. So, on which side should someone who takes ethics seriously come down? How important is expert knowledge – to what extent should it guide the decisions we make? Who has the burden of proof?

Where there is a situation that could be negatively affected by a proposed change, isn't it important that the proponent be able to show that either the action will not worsen existing conditions, that the possible change is justified by the result, or that the adverse condition can be contained? Otherwise, the Christian ethicist must reject the proposed change.

The issue is not unlike that of mine safety. In years past, mine tragedies were a fairly common occurrence, resulting in hard fought battles to require installation of safety features to prevent cave ins and explosions. Such tragedies are less frequent today but do occur, as happened in the Upper Big Branch Mine in West Virginia in 2010, where the company sacrificed safety regulations for profits, resulting in an explosion that killed 29 miners.

In the modern world, there are means of protecting people from harm that did not exist even a hundred years ago. The air pollution in cities like Beijing and New Delhi could be mitigated, if not eliminated, by inhibiting traffic and shutting down coal-fired power plants. Those measures would be costly and would entail much public objection. So, there is a trade-off between risk and economic security. It's not easy to grapple with these issues – but thoughtful people who take their ethical (Christian) responsibility seriously need to strive to work out reasonable answers.

Some who call themselves Christians have taken the position that the Last Judgment is near and that the condition of the environment just doesn't matter. These unfortunate people have shirked their responsibility to the earth which they inherited. They have deluded themselves since those expecting the Last Judgement have been looking for it for the last two thousand years – and even before that. Evading responsibility for the condition of the earth is contrary to the Psalmists observation that "the earth is the Lord's and the fullness thereof." Taking care of the earth is a fulfillment of the responsibility given to us by the Lord. Those who shirk that responsibility are neglecting the charge given to them.

LEGAL JUSTICE & CRIMINALITY: THE CRIMINAL, INCARCERATION, & CAPITAL PUNISHMENT

The Meaning and Purpose of Convicting and Sentencing the Guilty

The purpose of imprisonment is (1) punishment as a consequence of one's actions and as an incentive not to repeat the behavior, (2) removal from society, at least temporarily, so that the convict can do no further harm, and (3) rehabilitation, to teach the offender some skills to eventually reenter society in a constructive manner.

Generally speaking, prisons are a terrible environment to endure for anyone because of the lawlessness that goes on within. The prisoner is subject to violence within that far exceeds the punishment for which he/ she is sentenced. While prisons perform the first and second objectives, they are less successful at rehabilitation. Recidivism rates are high, although some innovative techniques have proven successful in reducing subsequent criminal behaviors. While serving time in prisons, the convict is subjected to harsh treatment, both by fellow prisoners and by the guard staff who may go beyond their need to behave in a defensive way for their self-protection, often expressing itself in brutal behavior against angry prisoners. Prisoners are largely out of sight and the way they are treated is largely unknown to the public on the outside.

For most people in America, the objectives of punishment and segregating the prisoner from society are more important than is the intent to provide the opportunity for education, treatment and rehabilitation. A prisoner is still a human being and needs to be treated with dignity and respect, features usually lacking in the prison environment. Those who try to give the prisoner support are often vilified by prison attendants.

The Danger of Convicting the Innocent

There is always the danger of apprehending, convicting and incarcerating the innocent. Everyone has had the misfortune of being falsely accused of a minor offense – and the outrage of knowing one's innocence. When that offense is a criminal offense, resulting in a fine or imprisonment, one's sense of outrage is vastly heightened. When the punishment is lengthy and severe, and lasts into the future following release, one hungers for justice, for exoneration. "Won't someone help me?" is the cry.

One's guilt for a crime may also have to do with the circumstances of the act – or with one's mental condition – or with some other aspect of the situation that juries never find out about that should be considered in determining the guilt of the accused. Extenuating circumstances can mitigate one's guilt – and justify release.

Justice is not always available. It is not always achieved. There are wrongs that go unpunished – and there are innocents who are never relieved of their suffering. Despite that reality, there is always the opportunity – the possibility – for being comforted, for acceptance, for compassion, for mercy.

So, what does Christian ethics say about people who are convicted of crimes but still proclaim their innocence, knowing that many guilty people, nonetheless, proclaim their innocence? Some are sociopaths, skilled at manipulating and hoodwinking others. At the same time, some are truly innocent. They all are people. Shall we simply dismiss them and leave them to be dealt with by government officials?

The Death Penalty

Opposition to the death penalty seems to be strongest among church leaders and clergy, even though many church people seem to feel its continuation – or at least its potential – is appropriate for certain crimes. In defense of the death penalty, it has to be recognized that there have been – and will be – those who perpetrate horrendous crimes and brutalities against others that it is hard not to see why they should not be eliminated from our midst. You could name many others in addition to Adolf Hitler and Saddam Hussein who have been responsible for the deaths of tens, hundreds, thousands and even millions of people who do not deserve to live. Theirs are not merely sins of omission but sins of commission that would justify their execution.

The problem is: what if the courts make a mistake? What if an innocent person is executed? Who, then, has committed the crime, the sin? The Innocence Project has found many cases now that have exonerated the innocent, people who have been incarcerated – and many executed – for crimes that they clearly, in retrospect, did not commit. If justice is a prime criteria, how can justice be obtained if there is a death penalty in place? Would it not be better to keep a bestial criminal alive – even in prison - rather than execute the innocent? Where is justice? How do you know with absolute certainty that someone is guilty as charged – or even that there were not mitigating circumstances? Or, conversely, is justice served by allowing a horrendous killer to continue to live?

The Hebrew Scriptures are clear evidence of the difficulty for finding justice. David, for example, was guilty of the genocide of several tribes that were conquered in the military campaign for Jerusalem. Yet, he was never held accountable for these killings while others were brought to justice for their lesser crimes. The Bible is ambiguous about justice.

Sentencing Appropriate for the Crime

Society's determined punishment for a crime may exceed what is justified – or it may be too lenient. Presidents commonly pardon people who have been given harsh sentences for crimes committed, having, in their judgment, received undeserved sentences or having fulfilled their obligation in the sentences already endured. In law, it is always an ongoing search to find and enact penalties appropriate for crimes committed – and those penalties are revised from time to time. Christian ethics challenges society to carry on this search, using fairness, civility, understanding, empathy and compassion as its criteria. The great problem is that the law imposes penalties by category, whereas, for the Christian, the penalty should be imposed on a person by person basis. But, then, who decides the fate of another? Judges impose penalties – but judges are not consistent with one another – and fairness is elusive.

Sentencing Alternatives

There are those who violate their own humanity by robbing and harming others. Some are desperate, some are captive of their own emotions, some are sociopathic and non-empathetic with others they would take advantage of. Society punishes them in the way it knows how: it puts them into prison. With more than 2.3 million people behind bars in the US today, the United States leads the world in both the number and percentage of residents it incarcerates, leaving far-more-populous China a distant second, according to a study by the nonpartisan Pew Center on the States.

The growth in prison population is largely because of tougher state and federal sentencing imposed since the mid-1980s. Minorities have been particularly affected: One in nine black men ages 20 to 34 is behind bars. For black women ages 35 to 39, the figure is one in 100, compared with one in 355 for white women in the same age group.

Punishment and incarceration as a consequence of one's criminal actions and as an incentive not to repeat the behavior is a form of social control. Because of the high recidivism rate, it is largely ineffective for that purpose. In removing the criminal from society, if only temporarily, presumably the convict can do no further harm. That, perhaps, is a good thing although it does not help him/her to learn to live productively and cooperatively in the real world. Rehabilitation should probably be the primary objective (from an ethical perspective) to teach the offender the skills to eventually reenter society in a constructive manner.

In April 2017, on CBS 60 Minutes, Ninth Circuit Court Judge Alex Kozinski claimed that probably 1% of people in prison are actually innocent of the crimes for which they were convicted. That's at least 23,000 people sitting in prison, innocent of the crimes for which they were committed. At the same time, Kozinski stated that he supported the death penalty for those convicted of extremely serious crimes. In other words, Kozinski is saying that 1% of those convicted of crimes deserving execution should not be executed. How do you make sense of that?

• **This is prison? 60 Minutes goes to Germany**   2016 Mar 31

Germany's prison system keeps convicts comfortable, costs less and has lower recidivism rates - but would Americans ever accept it?

In Germany, prison isn't meant to punish, it's designed to mirror normal life as much as possible. Among the privileges enjoyed by German prisoners: immaculate facilities, organized sports, video games and keys to their own cells. Inmates can wear street clothes and can freely decorate their own cells – keeping all sorts of household objects that American prison guards might consider dangerous. Prisoners who demonstrate good behavior can even leave prison for work or weekend getaways. Average Americans may balk at this level of freedom for convicted criminals, but prisons in Germany cost less and produce far fewer repeat offenders than U.S. prisons. Reporter Bill Whitaker reports on a corrections concept that may shock Americans but could offer solutions for the troubled U.S. system.

In Germany, 75 percent of prisoners sentenced to life are paroled after 20 years or less, even Bernd Junge, a contract killer who shot a woman to death. Should Junge, who Whitaker meets on an unsupervised weekend furlough, be offered a future? "Yes, he should," says Joerg Jesse, a psychologist and the director of prisons in the German state of Mecklenburg-Western Pomerania. Jesse says German inmates deserve rehabilitation, not retribution, during their prison stays.

"The real goal is re-integration into society, train them to find a different way to handle their situation outside, life without further crimes, life without creating new victims," says Jesse. "We cannot see the sense in just locking people up for their whole life. Your prisons will fill up and you'll have to build new prisons and so on and I think that was the situation in the U.S."

The U.S. makes up just five percent of the world's population but incarcerates 25 percent of the world's prisoners. Whitaker reports that American politicians and prison officials are visiting German prisons looking for ideas they can take home. On a tour of a Berlin prison, Whitaker meets Connecticut Gov. Dannel Malloy. He was impressed with the German results. "I think there are many things that are transferable. That doesn't mean that it's a perfect fit. But I think we have to challenge ourselves to do better," Malloy tells Whitaker.

Pennsylvania's Secretary of Corrections, John Wetzel, began work in his state's system three decades ago. Back in 1980, there were 8,000 inmates in the state. Today, there are 50,000. Wetzel has seen Germany's system, too. "Frankly [we] screwed up the corrections system for 30 years and it's time to do something different. It really starts with understanding...a human-being's value isn't diminished by being incarcerated," says Wetzel.

Wetzel would like prisons in the U.S. to look more like prisons in Germany, but he also understands how hard it will be to convince the majority of Americans that a more lenient penal system can work. "It's crossing the Grand Canyon that we're talking about".

Generally speaking, prisons are a terrible environment to endure for anyone because of the lawlessness that goes on within. The prisoner is subject to violence within that far exceeds the punishment for which he/she is sentenced. While prisons perform the objectives of punishment and incarceration, they are less successful at rehabilitation. Recidivism rates are high, although some innovative techniques have proven successful in reducing subsequent criminal behaviors. While serving time in prisons, the convict is subjected to harsh treatment, both by fellow prisoners and by the guard staff who may go beyond their need to enforce proper behavior as a defense for their self-protection, often expressing itself in brutal activity against angry prisoners. Prisoners are largely out of sight and their treatment is largely unknown to the public on the outside.

For society outside of prison in America, the objectives of punishment and segregating the prisoner from society are more important than is the intent to provide the opportunity for education, treatment and rehabilitation. A prisoner is still a human being and needs to be treated with dignity and respect, a feature that is usually lacking in the prison environment. Those who try to give the prisoner support are often vilified by prison attendants.

It is interesting to note that prisoners in some European countries (notably Germany) find themselves in a more constructive environment and that, having served their time, recidivism rates of prisoners are considerably lower than in the U.S. Where this model exists demonstrates the effectiveness of affirming the human dignity of people, even in difficult circumstances. Such a model is more in accord with a position informed by Christian ethics.

Because the more punitive model has prevailed for so long, implementation of the European model meets resistance from the existing bureaucracies elsewhere (including America), although some progressive voices are doing their best to change the system, if only because it provides a safer environment for those who must administer the prison system – and because it offers the hope that prisoners can see some positive potential for their lives after completion of their sentences.

Prison reform should be an important issue for those who aspire to make a positive influence in a society that tends to forget the locked-away prisoners who are out of sight. And, yet, it is precisely because they are invisible that they should be of concern to those who care about the prevalence of a Christian ethic. It is incumbent on Christians to seek the rehabilitation of those who can be rehabilitated. Prison ministries usually try to do that. Problem is: there aren't enough of them.

HEALTH CARE

Some have asserted that effective health care is a human right, that no one should be deprived of the best care available because of money, or access, or any other condition, that the impoverished person is just as worthy of the best care as the wealthiest person. If a Christian ethic means anything, it must support this view and see to it that the most generous and effective health care legislation is generous and is implemented. Attending to the sick and ill was an important priority for Jesus. It should be for modern day Christians as well.

CONTAGION

Periodically throughout history, contagious diseases have wrought havoc with human populations. During the Middle Ages, it is thought that 30 to 60% of the population of Europe, 75 to 200 million people in Eurasia and peaking in Europe in the years 1346–1353, died of the Black Death. In her book, *The Coming Plague (1994),* Laurie Garrett chronicles the many types of diseases that could evolve into devastating plagues for humankind. Since publication of her book, swine flu and Legionnaires disease, AIDS, Ebola and, more recently, COVID-19 have threatened but have been held in check. It is incumbent that these deadly threats be prevented from spreading.

These potentially devastating diseases usually appear in certain distant parts of the world and then migrate to other areas. The usual response is to contain the outbreak to particular areas, such as Ebola in central Africa. It's not uncommon for the attitude of Westerners to be unconcerned, as long as the health threat is contained in a distant location, I don't need to be concerned. That's hardly an ethical response, to be unconcerned about the devastation the outbreak has when occurring elsewhere – but the COVID-19 pandemic could change that attitude. Christian ethics is not confined to concern just for any one place, or country, or part of the world. It is universal in its concern for people everywhere. A contagion in Uganda is as much of a concern for the people whose lives will be affected there as it would be if a child down the street ls stricken. The motivation of a Christian ethical concern is as much a concern for the people in distant places as it is for one's own safety and security.

VACCINATION

A dispute has been going on for several years over the use of vaccination as a preventative of contagious diseases. Health authorities are almost unanimous in agreement over the efficacy of vaccination. But, there are those, including a few medical specialists, who contend that vaccinations can lead to autism and who therefore oppose their use.

This is an important issue in the community since the diseases that are usually subject to vaccination are mumps, measles, whooping cough, flu and chicken pox, each of which can cause severe symptoms, even an occasional death. And, because they are contagious, can spread from one child to another and affect an entire local community. A parent who is concerned about the health of the child and the community may feel there is a difficult choice to make. Can a Christian ethic have relevance in such a situation?

Certainly, the health of the community is of great importance – but a parent who is concerned about child health in general also and rightfully regards their own child's health as of great importance. What needs to occur in such a situation is for the people involved to enter into a conversation as to how, together, they can find ways to insure everyone's health without one dominating the other.

CONTRACEPTION

Despite the availability of birth control since the middle of the 19th century, and the development of the contraceptive pill in the mid-twentieth century, the argument over contraception persists, with some contending that it is immoral to use any method whatsoever to interfere with "the will of God". Others argue that family planning with the use of contraceptives is a more responsible way to bring a child into the world and protect the health of women. The ethical issue here has been largely won by the latter argument. Nonetheless, the issue should remain open for discussion.

ABORTION

A child is conceived and grows in the womb – until its life is snuffed out in a medical procedure called abortion. The mother may matter-of-factly not wish to be burdened with the gestation period, let alone the responsibility for raising the child. Or, the mother may be in great emotional distress about her inability to care for the child or her fear of telling her parents – or, the child may be deformed and pose a huge burden upon the parents in caring for a helpless infant, growing older into an adult needing constant care.

Not many years ago, being pregnant with an out-of-wedlock child was socially unacceptable. It mandated that the mother would disappear for a few months to another community – or that the mother would experience ostracism or rejection. Oftentimes, the couple would be forced into a marriage that neither wanted nor could maintain – or it would result in a woman getting a dangerous abortion from an unqualified and unsanitary abortionist. It was a horrendous emotional experience that a woman would suffer. Unmarried pregnancies are now much more acceptable but still represent an emotional trial for most unmarried mothers – or mothers of impaired fetuses.

There are those who oppose abortion as a procedure because they argue that a person is created at conception and is therefore being murdered in an abortion procedure. There are others who feel that the mother is a victim of a society that chooses to take charge of her womb – and that an abortion is a compassionate response for the mother to make. And, there are those who argue that no woman should be forced to give birth to an unwanted child or a child who is deformed, who is otherwise impaired or who is conceived in a rape – or even by accident.

The issue is further defined by the opposition of a mostly male contingent arguing against abortions for a completely subdominant group of women. Why should men have the right to say that women who conceive should have to undergo their nine-month pregnancies and then have to decide what to do with their newborn child? Were it left to women alone, there would be no question as to the outcome, despite the fact that there are some women in the anti-abortion movement.

Where would Jesus come out on this one? It's hard to say, for he certainly had compassion for children. And yet, whenever he interacted with women, as in his encounter with the Samaritan woman at the well, he clearly gave them non-judgmental support. He understood their difficult role in a society in which men dominated and acted judgmentally toward women. When a woman was threatened with stoning for an adulterous affair, he again stepped in to defend her.

The argument that anti-abortionists raise is the issue of human life at conception – and the importance of preserving it. Pro-choice advocates do not discount the importance of the fetus but argue that it attains personhood only at birth – and only with out-of-womb experience. They argue that the woman bearing the child has the right to make the decision as to whether or not to bring that child to birth and that it is not the right of the government to force that decision on the woman in any particular way, either to be forced to conceive (by a certain age) or to abort a fetus.

Anti-abortionists argue that the soul of a person results from the fertilization of the ovum (egg) and that any interference with the development of the resulting fetus constitutes murder. Pro-choice advocates dismiss that argument and contend that a fetus that cannot survive outside the womb is not yet more than a collection of cellular material. Most feel that once the fetus achieves independent survivability (at five or six months), it then deserves protection unless it is deformed or has died.

Alternatively, pro-choice advocates point to the situation that stillborn fetuses or fetuses aborted before viability are rarely named or buried and have been accorded none of the necessary characteristics of a human. Christian ethics argues that children born into unsupportive situations where they are neglected, resented, treated harshly or malnourished suffer both mentally and physically and would be better off if they had not been born. Furthermore, there is the ethical argument that the physical and mental health of the pregnant woman deserves the greater importance, more so than the right of the fetus to survive. Should the woman desire to abort the fetus, it should be her right to do so. Those who support her are not "pro-abortion". They are "pro-woman". They support a woman's right to make the decision about her health, her future and whether a fetus should become a person, oftentimes dependent upon her alone. That a man (or men) who does not have the burden of carrying the unborn fetus, should have the right to make this decision over another person is clearly unethical. For the woman, it can be an emotionally difficult decision for which she deserves understanding and compassionate support.

The controversy over abortion has been largely waged over these grounds – and seems to have a social class relationship as well as a religious one. Here in the U.S. in the 1950s, abortion was illegal but was commonly achieved under healthy conditions by people who could afford to pay for a reputable doctor and clinic. Poorer clients had to find an abortion provider who may or may not have been a competent physician and where the clinical conditions were often unsafe. It was not uncommon for these abortions to lead to complications, health problems and even deaths.

The Supreme Court case, Roe vs. Wade in 1973, made abortion legal although, depending on the situation, varying in the ability to achieve. In the time since it was decided, it has come increasingly under attack by those who argue that abortion is immoral, and that Roe should be overturned. In the meantime, some states have introduced laws that make it more difficult for a woman to obtain an abortion. For the Christian ethicist, it is an important issue and consists of many facets.

DOCTOR-ASSISTED SUICIDE

Does a Christian ethic mean that one must endure a miserable, painful existence while he/she waits for nature to run its course to end one's life? Can one ethically decide to end his/her life? What is the compassionate, sensible thing to do for a person who is in pain and terminal? The Gospels indicate that Jesus expected people to take responsibility for their lives, although others (self-appointed authorities) may try to make decisions for them. There is no easy answer to these questions – but understanding and empathy are the appropriate attitudes to take in difficult situations.

EUTHANASIA

Perhaps the more difficult question is whether someone who is seriously ill, even comatose, with no hope for recovery, should be allowed to perish by removal of life-sustaining equipment or even be given an injection to end his/her life. The law aside, is it ethical to keep a comatose person alive when there is no hope of recovery? On occasion, family members and medical personnel must make these kinds of decisions. What one can say about Christian ethics is that it is permissive, not prescriptive or authoritarian. Where hard choices are involved, it has no hard, fast and inflexible rules. It prescribes one to use compassion and good judgment – and is unwilling to condemn when care, concern and understanding are involved. In any case, what is paramount is to advocate the development of procedures that will protect patients against abuse.

13

OTHER SOCIAL JUSTICE ISSUES TODAY

I t has been the role of the church to limit the issues that it considers itself competent to address. For the first part of the 19th century, at least in the North, it was slavery. Following the Civil War, the Protestant churches addressed the issue of alcoholism and supported Prohibition. To a lesser degree, the rights of labor and the fight for women's suffrage were supported by the churches. In some churches, dancing was considered sinful until the mid-19050s. But, sexual profligacy was a prime issue in the churches throughout most of the 20th century. Billy Graham railed against divorce as an indicator of the deterioration of civilized society (even though two of his children have since been divorced). More recently, several mainline churches have opposed the death penalty as a necessary punishment for those convicted of the most serious crimes. But, churches have been reluctant to address more controversial issues in society – or even to discuss them as ethical issues.

THE IMPORTANCE OF AN ETHICAL APPROACH: A CHRISTIAN IDEAL FOR SOCIETY

The saga of human history is a narrative of the difficulty of people to live successfully with one another. It's told in the fable of Adam and Eve and their sons, Cain and Abel. It's the story of the Tower of Babel, the story of Jacob and Esau, the tale of the sons of Jacob and how they sold their brother, Joseph, into slavery in Egypt. It's the story of the Jews in Egypt and how the Egyptians turned against them – and then of how the Jews returned to Canaan to drive out the Philistines. It's the story of small battles and great wars – and the difficulty of countries to abide with each other. It's the story of people and countries trying to find a way toward accommodation.

The search for a universal ethic has always been difficult because of those who claim superior rights over others. It shouldn't be that difficult to achieve an agreement on how to live peacefully together and to minimize the tendencies of some people to want to claim an advantage over others, too often in a very hostile way. Finding an ethic that all people can accept as their own best way of living in community is essential if strife and discord are to be avoided. In his small community of the first century, it is what Jesus sought to identify. In our world of seven billion people, involving far more complexities than Jesus confronted in his day, it is still our necessary goal. To the extent that we can find and pursue it, it is our chosen way to live. While it is a Christian pursuit, it is a universal pursuit as well, to find and practice a common ethic for the entire earth.

JUSTICE & DEMOCRACY

There seems to be some pushback currently against the movement for democracy throughout the world, the notion of people governing themselves. The Greeks, for a short time 2,500 years ago, experimented with a male-dominated democracy – but then gave up on the idea. It languished in the shadows for centuries, with occasional eruptions in the intervening years. New Englanders, for a time, practiced a radical democracy with town meeting government in the seventeenth century – but, as populations swelled, realized the impracticality of direct democracy in governments larger than the small town entity. Based on the desire for justice, the idea of government evolved into representative (republican) government. Nonetheless, the notion has persisted that ultimate political power should reside with the people, ALL of the people of qualifying age, regardless of gender, race, religion or property ownership.

The democratic idea evolved from the concept of basic human rights, that all are created equal (from a political perspective) and deserve the right to create their own destinies. It is an idea that evolved out of the Christian understanding of who each person is, equal in the eyes of God. At the same time, every human lives in a community of other humans and is obligated to respect the humanity of the other person – and of the community in which they share living space. Justice is the fundamental idea underlying democratic government, the realization that there must be an impartial determinant that defends human and civil rights – and provides for the general welfare of the community it serves.

A democracy that respects the human political rights of each person is the inevitable outcome of a Christian understanding of humanity. While laws and mutual respect may improve limits on an individual's freedom, they do not impair the respect we must have for one another – although aberrant or criminal behavior may require restraint of certain individuals. But, with respect to government, a democratic form, even a representative (republican) democracy, is what is called for – is what is appropriate – and the goal of an ethical form of government.

HUMANITARIAN ISSUES

Animal Rights/Animal Welfare/Treatment of Animals

Perhaps animal abuse is not as common as it once was – but it still occurs more often that we would like to admit. St. Francis (13th century) is known and renowned for his love of animals, regarding them as elements of the revered creation. But, empathy for the welfare of animals did not take organizational form until the 1820s in England when the first SPCA society was founded. Of course, it can be surmised that people have long experienced empathy for the welfare of animals, especially pets, but did not consider such sentiments could be expressed in a social movement until early in the 19th century. Organizations such as the local chapters of the SPCA and the Humane Society of the U.S. (HSUS) have been around for a long time, working to eliminate animal cruelty.

The values that shaped HSUS's formation in 1954, came in some degree from the humane movement that originated in the 1860s in the United States. The idea of kindness to animals made significant inroads in American culture in the years following the Civil War. The development of sympathy for creatures in pain, the satisfaction of keeping them as pets, and the heightening awareness about the relationship between cruelty to animals and interpersonal violence strengthened the movement's popular appeal.

The most immediate philosophical influence on 1950s-era advocates was the reverence-for-life concept advanced years earlier by Albert Schweitzer, a concept that emerged from his theological convictions as a Christian theologian. Schweitzer included a deep regard for nonhuman animals in his canon of beliefs, and animal advocates laboring to give their concerns a higher profile were buoyed by Schweitzer's 1952 Nobel Peace Prize speech, in which he noted that "compassion, in which ethics takes root, does not assume its true proportions until it embraces not only man but every living being".

In an ethical sense, mistreatment of animals, animal cruelty, is not unlike cruelty of one human for another. There have been studies that have found that people who treat others abusively often have abused animals, pets and others, as children. Our laws have been developed with respect to inter-human relations but have more recently come to apply to domesticated animals. Society reasons that animal cruelty causes inexcusable physical and mental pain that cannot be tolerated, even though pets are possessions of people and do not independently have the same legal rights as people. Unfortunately, cruelty laws do not apply to wildlife and cruel animal traps are legal in most states.

As noted elsewhere, empathy is an essential Christian trait, empathy for the tribulation, anguish and pain of other people – an attitude that could extend to other creatures, even snakes and mice and other undesirables. Perhaps other life forms need to be included for those who are accorded empathy. The way we treat other creatures is an indication of who we are and how we regard the world.

Refugees: The Poor & Oppressed

Refugees have tended to be forgotten people as well. But, those who find themselves as refugees in the world, displaced from their homes, have grown dramatically in numbers in the recent past. There are more than 18 million refugees in the world today. This is a dramatic increase since the mid-1970s when there were less than 5 million refugees worldwide. At any one time throughout the year, approximately 60 million people are driven from their homes.

Consider the life of a refugee. There is no home to go to that you can call your own, that you can rely on to be there for the coming night, where you can keep your clothing and possessions and have a place to store and cook your food. You might be living in a tent with little protection against the cold. You have no security against those who may want to rob or harm you or your children; you may be forced to pick up and move at any moment, needing to walk long distances over difficult terrain and in the cold. The water where you are could be unclean. You must rely on an NGO to provide you with food – and it may be food you'd throw away at normal times. There may be no medical or toileting facilities. Educational opportunities for your children are sparse; your children are dirty and hungry – and there's nothing you can do about it. There is no work, no resources to make a little money, no way to provide for yourself. You are totally dependent on the good will of others. Can you see yourself in such a situation?

Sixty million people – even just 18 million people - is a lot of people, people Christians must acknowledge who have as much intrinsic value as anyone. Most live a long way away, across the oceans, in hard to reach places. Whereas once these refugees were impossible to reach, today, there are service agencies (NGOs) that can now provide some level of care. Nonetheless, the task is enormous, even for these agencies to meet a minimum of need, let alone for a wealthy individual to respond with any effectiveness. Churches are likewise impotent. The only significant institutions capable of providing help to refugee populations are governments who have the money and resources to make an impact.

Christians can stand idly by and observe the refugee calamity – or they can become involved by pressuring their governments to come to the aid of these people. Too often, affluent populations are resistant to spending their tax dollars to help the invisible, impoverished, distant refugees. Christians, through their missions, can try to meet specific challenges – but their resources are limited. Government attention and support are essential. Christians can do what they can to see to it that government assistance is effectively and efficiently provided.

Immigration

The immigration issue is closely tied to the refugee question. People migrate to another country for a variety of reasons: for business opportunities, to enjoy a more affluent lifestyle, to join family members who have immigrated previously, to improve their job opportunities, for aesthetic reasons, for health reasons, but also to escape poverty and danger. There has developed in the United States an attitude about who should be allowed to immigrate. Some we welcome, others we do not. It is common to feel that people with technical skills should be allowed but those without skills should be kept away. The common belief and argument are that those who cross the border illegally, for whatever reason, should be deported back to the country from whence they came. But, what should the attitude of the Christian be toward those who are desperate and fear for their lives, even if they are illegal entrants?

There are some Christian churches that have taken up the practice of providing "sanctuary" for those who would otherwise be deported, feeling that it is the ethical charge, feeling it is the mission, of the Christian to provide for those who are suffering discrimination and persecution and danger. Some of those the government wishes to deport have come into the U.S. as children and know no other country as home. Some face danger if returned to their native countries, even the prospect of being killed by gangs of thugs. Some have fled poverty to gain meager employment to earn a few dollars that can be sent back to aid family members. Others are trying to keep their families together. Some just want a better life.

What a Christian ethic says about these immigrants who face deportation tends to lean on the side of providing "sanctuary". That's not to say that there are not situations of abuse or evasion or criminal activity or legitimate reasons for not providing sanctuary. But, it is to say that there is an ethical responsibility that cannot be denied and that Christians are charged with observing.

Indigenous Peoples – Native Americans

It is difficult to understand how the early Europeans, bearing the banner of Christ, could impose on the natives of America the atrocities that they perpetrated. Columbus enslaved the natives of Hispaniola. The Spanish conquistadores of Mexico and Central America fought and murdered the Aztecs and Mayan natives who welcomed them and regarded them as gods. The early settlers of Virginia and Massachusetts encroached upon the natives of those areas and drove them away. All brought European diseases that infected the native people who died by the thousands (if not the millions). The natives were regarded as competitors and enemies – and cruelly decimated. Military forces of the United States drove the Indians further to the west, deprived them of the buffalo on which their lives depended, occasionally massacred them. then confined them to reservations on land no longer wanted by whites. This was the sad saga of what happened to the Indians of America perpetrated by the "Christian" invaders from Europe who were oblivious of the compassion mandated by the Jesus whom they professed to follow.

Nothing can assuage the crimes perpetrated by "Christians" of the past against the native peoples of America, of Africa, of Asia and Australia. But, we are the inheritors of that legacy and must be aware of what we have inherited – and do our best to avoid perpetrating further crimes of a similar nature and attempt to rectify those wrongs as they persist into this day. A Christian ethic for the modern day means that native peoples are regarded with respect, recognize how the crimes of the past have persisted into this day, and find ways to make up for those iniquities. Christian congregations owe the hand of friendship and support to the descendants of the natives who were so terribly abused. Whether in legislation that affects them or in local policies that relate to them, it is important that Americans recognize that imperative – for these people are our brothers and sisters and we owe them much.

Sexual Exploitation of Adults, Elder Abuse, Spousal Abuse

Christian ethics begins with the belief that it is not normal or healthy for a person to abuse others since abuse of others, sexual or otherwise, violates the humanity of the abused. Sexual abuse is rooted in the unhealthy mental and emotional psyche of the abuser. People who are abusers have often endured sexual abuse themselves – and have reacted accordingly. Thus, the ethical and psychological issues involved in abuse converge with each other and are difficult to separate. This leads to the conclusion that the moral issue surrounding abuse has a psychological root that must be treated as a health issue while being condemned from

an ethical perspective. When abuse occurs, it needs to be punished as a criminal offense, even though the perpetrator is emotionally or mentally defective. Whether people who are sexually abusive can be treated and "cured" isn't clear at this time. Professionals are currently in disagreement.

Current practice allows sexual offenders to be released into society, although stigmatized by the requirement that they be registered as sexual offenders and neighbors notified of their presence nearby.

From a Christian ethical perspective, victims of sexual predators deserve understanding, support and reassurance. This is the priority response. But, perpetrators also need help to recover as best possible, separate themselves from dangerous situations and find ways to lead normal lives. To be outcast and forgotten is a cruel and wasteful punishment. It is the challenge to Christians to find ways to redeem, heal, recover and restore those who are ill and afflicted.

ECONOMIC POLICY, LABOR ISSUES & JUSTICE

Christian ethics requires that people be treated equitably and fairly – and that the society that provides support for the poor is a just society. Those basic elements of support are nourishment, shelter, education and health care. Again, using the Parable of the Good Samaritan, it is simply immoral to ignore those who are beaten down and abandoned (by society), whether due to their own fault or by others. We do this for medical emergencies. Food banks exist in many communities. And, in most places, you will even find homeless shelters. Sometimes these are funded with public money – but not everywhere. These, however, are stopgap measures and do not really address the importance of integrating the needy into the economic structure of society.

The mutual benefit economy of the early Christian community (Acts chs. 4 & 5) apparently did not work for long and eventually dissolved. Nonetheless, it served as a model of the caring community that is to be sought by Christians, at least for one another. It suggests

a model for the larger society, that it be organized to provide basic support for everyone. In the developed world of the 21st century, it is done reasonably well. Some communities do better than others. Some countries do better than others. Where there is no political structure that provides support, or where it is done poorly, the destitute must rely on personal or private charity (i.e. begging for handouts).

It would be better if the economic structure were arranged so that everyone could participate, everyone who wished to could work (for a livable wage) and those who can't work were adequately provided for. This is the kind of society the Christian should strive to create and provide. But, there are inequities that cry out for redress.

Economic Justice

No society has found a way to provide economic justice for all of its members. There has always been a gap between the wealthy and the poor. As Jesus said, "The poor you will always have with you." But the opposite is also true, the undeserving wealthy will always be with you. It's just that circumstances have changed, and the numbers of the poor are far greater than ever. Too many people are born into poverty – and never escape it. But, children are born into wealthy families – and never escape their wealth, even though they never earned it. Is either situation right? Is either situation fair? Can either situation ever be morally justified?

If wealth is a good thing, Fortune smiles on some by being born into it. Others obtain wealth by their brilliance, hard work, or just good luck, being in the right place at the right time and doing what needs to be done. If they achieve wealth during their lifetimes, they pass it on to their children, who did nothing to gain wealth except to be born to the right parents. Some of them use it to gain more wealth or at least to sustain themselves. Some use it up or abuse it and just throw it away. Even this is fortuitous. At the time of the Depression in 1929-30, there were large fortunes that disappeared within a few days, all because someone was invested in the wrong thing at the wrong time. One's

merit had nothing to do with it. It just happened. One day wealthy; the next day insolvent.

But, then, there is poverty – the poor. One could be brilliant and achieve much – a musician or a scientist - if given the opportunity to have an instrument – or an education – or access to a laboratory. But, poverty can destroy that opportunity. Consider the American slave who might have been smart and achieved much, but was forced to work in the fields, day after day, from the time he/she was a toddler. Economic justice suggests that everyone be accorded some opportunity to escape the burden of poverty – and lead a sufficient – if not optimal - life.

The moral position – the Christian position – is that every person deserves such an opportunity to lead an optimal life, that wealth can be destructive of one's moral sensitivity to this egalitarian perspective. Reflecting this moral obligation, Jesus told the Rich Young Ruler to "Go sell, all that you have, give it to the poor, and come, follow me." (Mt. 19:16-30). But, the tendency of the Wealthy is to hoard their wealth or to spend it in frivolous living and to pass it on to their children.

The accumulation of wealth is not the issue here. Wealth sometimes just happens fortuitously – or even because of one's diligence or hard work. The wealthy are fortunate in this commendable sense: they can use their wealth to create great works of art - or science – or engineering. They can use it in ways to fund educational and university projects, museums, pet sanctuaries, homes for the disabled or aged, wildlife sanctuaries, parks and libraries. They can fund civil rights organizations, humane societies, scholarship programs, or medical research.

There are innumerable ways the wealthy can make a contribution to the betterment of human life. But, passing on extraordinary wealth to one's children is hardly justifiable.

Labor

Most people must work in order to earn a living. Some people work in order to accomplish some goal in life. Other people work in order to occupy their time but without any particular objective in mind.

Some people do not need to work – and don't. The best kind of work is purposeful, done to achieve some goal. Some people get great personal satisfaction out of their work. Other people hate their work. Some people are exploited and find themselves taken advantage of – but have no alternative than to continue working, even though they are inadequately compensated. Other people are overly compensated for what they do. The marketplace is supposed to compensate fairly for what they do, but compensation is arbitrary and rarely fair. When laborers are few, employers are willing to pay excessive wages to get workers. When laborers are plentiful and compete with one another for jobs, employers will find the cheapest labor they can get.

In his *Little Blue Book*, George Lakoff divides workers between asset workers, "the most valued people… who are given stock options, respected, treated well and paid well with salaries…" - and resource workers, "on a par with material resources like steel and fuel, to be used efficiently and exploited maximally at minimal cost. They are central to profit creation, yet they get little or no respect, are interchangeable, and are paid as little as possible with wages. Individually they are powerless, and so they perform best, and cost the corporation the most, when represented by a union. Asset employees tend not to be represented by unions since they are inherently valued". Since "health care coverage and pensions make up part of the pay earned by workers", "Corporations have an ethical responsibility to pay *in full* for work done."

The willingness for Christians to address labor injustice and seek honorable, fair and progressive working conditions has varied from time to time. Its most active time was during the late nineteenth and early 20th centuries when labor conditions were deplorable in this country, prompting workers to organize and form labor unions. The union movement was rough and angry, even violent at times (with management usually responding with violence, even initiating it at times) - but it offered workers a sense a self-worth and camaraderie – and the knowledge that they were fighting for justice. Even then, smug, wealthy churches took management's side of the argument or confined themselves to "spiritual" matters while the poorer churches sided with workers and the side of justice. It was the period when the Social Gospel movement was at its zenith.

Worker/Labor Exploitation

They are mostly gone now, but during the 19th century, as the United States was industrializing and expanding, there developed a system of worker exploitation that was demeaning and cruel, most notably in the mining industry but in other industries as well, such as forestry, agriculture & textiles. A worker would seek employment with a company that would rent housing to the worker and provide credit at the company store. So, the worker would be immediately indebted to the employer but not receive sufficient wages to extricate himself/herself from the debt, resulting in a situation that the worker was enslaved to the employer and could never be free. The employer held all the cards and could extract from the worker overbearing work in unsafe conditions. The situation continues to exist in some other countries – and even, to a small degree, here in the United States, especially where the worker does not have diverse skills and occupational choices.

This kind of exploitation is anathema to the Christian as completely unethical, since it is a form of slavery and aims at destroying the humanity of the worker. The Christian ethic aims to liberate the individual from domination by another person and to offer the right of self-determination and responsibility. Where such conditions exist, it is the role of the Christian to see that it is changed to a more equitable and humanizing one. The prophets railed against such exploitation by the wealthy against the poor as simply a righteously ethical mandate.

Perhaps this issue needs to be considered in the wider context of the wealth gap and what it means for society as a whole. In Jesus' day, the wealth gap we know about was between royalty – the Herods – and the common people. There were undoubtedly others who represented the wealthy elite such as "the Rich Young Ruler" and, perhaps, the temple authorities (the Sadducees) and the tax collectors. Jesus counseled against wealth as the foe of more important values – but he didn't seem to be aware of the social consequences of the wealth disparity on society. Nonetheless, they exist, and the Christian ethicist needs to recognize them.

The Poor & the Oppressed

The fishermen who Jesus called were not the social elite of first century Israeli society. In fact, they were close to the bottom tier and were mostly illiterate. But, they were the people he wanted to teach – and who could relate to the people he wanted to reach. The wealthy, the religious leaders, the social elite – these people were already leading self-satisfied lives. Jesus wanted to give those who had very little a modicum of justice and dignity, a sense of value of themselves as human beings. He sought to raise their spirits. The focus of his ministry was on the poor, the ill, the outcast.

Followers of Jesus are asked to pay attention to those who are poor and powerless, even those who are persecuted and oppressed. Oftentimes they are overlooked and unnoticed. They live in back alleys and obscure places where more secure people seldom, if ever, seem to go. They are the refugees and the homeless, the jobless and those without purpose or direction, the desperate and the criminal. They are the people no one cares about. They have always been out there – and they find life hard. In contemporary American society, they still exist. They are often vilified and scorned. The impulse is to ignore them and pretend, if not wish, that they do not exist. But they do exist. They are human. They do deserve our attention. There, but for the grace of God, go i.

In most Western societies, we have attempted to provide for these people, if only at a basic level. We do attempt to respond to the need that exists, whether caused by circumstance, by natural disasters, or by deliberate exclusion. It is important for followers of Jesus, those with an ethical concern for people and the environment in which they live, to attend to injustices and needs – and to attempt to rectify wrongs and to fill needs that exist.

Women's Pay Disparity

Could there be any justification for compensating a woman less for accomplishing the same work as a man? Why has this practice prevailed in many cultures in the past – and still prevails in some cultures today? Gender discrimination has the same underlying rationale as racial discrimination: the need of one class of people to dominate another, probably for economic reasons. It can hardly be justified.

A Christian ethic seeks equitability for everyone. Jesus saw no reason to discriminate and we find several places in the Gospels where he sought equality of women with men in a common humanity. Just because a cultural practice has survived from history's dark past does not mean it is right. When one group of people suffers unjustly at the hands of another group, it is a violation of the dignity of the members of that group. The practice has no ethical justification.

Pay Disparity Between Rich & Poor

Jesus had nothing to say about minimum wage requirements. In fact, a minimum wage was not decreed by law anywhere in the world until to 20th century and the New Deal in America. Previously market forces (or imperial decree) alone have determined what a worker would be paid. The question has always been what an employer was willing to pay to get a job done – or what a worker would accept (or demand) in order to take a job. Those with particular skills could always command a better wage than those without any specialized skill or talent.

In 1938, Congress established the initial minimum wage at 25 cents per hour. In 1968, it had increased to $ 1.75/hour (adjusted to $10.85/hour in current dollars) but it is now at $1.75/hour, so, in adjusted dollars, it has fallen). Some legislators want to eliminate it altogether. Anyway, a person needs to be working in order to get it.

Was it an ethical issue for government to establish a minimum wage in 1938? Is government responsible for establishing a wage that guarantees its workers a "livable" income? Does government have a responsibility for seeing that its members have some level of security in their lives, especially when some are flourishing while other seem to be falling between the cracks? Does government have a responsibility for seeing to it that its members have a basic standard of living? What should that be?

Until recently, most respondents would have answered "no" to those questions of governmental responsibility. And yet, the Constitution of the United States suggests otherwise. What should we conclude from a Christian ethical point of view?

Population

With seven to eight billion, we live in a much more populous and complex world than has even before been seen on the face of the earth, with far greater impact on what the earth can even sustain. The population of the world is increasing at a rate that it can be expected to double by the year 2100. The implications of this surge in population must be considered now by thoughtful people before the world becomes, for most of its people, unlivable. It is an issue for Christians to discuss within the context of their church communities.

Corporations: are They People?

In 2010, the U.S. Supreme Court, in its decision in the *Citizens United* case, gave corporations the status of persons, entitling corporations and labor unions to make the same unlimited political campaign contributions to Super PACs that individuals are entitled to make, in the process shooting down the prior acts of Congress that had limited such contributions as long as they were not coordinated directly with candidates running for office. The ruling gave corporations (with extensive resources) the green light to spend unlimited sums on ads and other political tools calling for the election or defeat of individual candidates.

American corporations are only about one hundred fifty years old that introduced the way of conducting business and followed the Civil War, the purpose of which was to shield business owners from exposure to bankruptcy. The corporation was developed as a business entity in its own right, subject to the laws imposed on it by the respective states and the Federal government. Although it could be sued for its misbehavior, it did not enjoy the rights conferred on citizens in the Bill of Rights: freedom of speech, religion, press, assembly, or the petition of government for a redress of grievances.

Corporate Power

The corporation hasn't always been around. It made its first appearance in the early 19th century but wasn't an important feature on the economic scene until the end of the century. It came into existence (1) in order to allow multiple owners to participate in the business by owning shares in the company, and (2) to protect the owners (i.e. shareholders) against personal liability for the company's business activities. The corporation isn't itself immoral. People can hold ownership in whatever way they choose. However, the practices of the company can be unethical – and that carries back to the owners themselves who allow the business to operate unethically.

Corporations have the ability to influence society – and the political life of that society – because of their size, resources and wealth. Their influence can have a negative (i.e. deleterious) effect upon the lives of people living in that society. Corporations need to be restrained so that their influence, deliberate or not, will not be harmful to people. Unfortunately, that responsibility can conflict with the influence its activities can have upon the owners who are seeking to be rewarded monetarily for their ownership. Where these conflicts arise, it is usual for the economic interests of the owners to prevail while the social interests of the community take the backseat.

Christian ethics takes the side of the larger community. It wants the company to survive and prosper since that will benefit the lives of its workers. But, its concerns are more far reaching than that. Suppose the company manufactures a product that is destructive of the environment in general or of a specific species of plant or animal. How is such a company justified to go on producing and sustaining jobs while the surrounding environment is degraded? Suppose the product the company manufactures is itself defective – for example, a seatbelt that breaks or releases, a food containing a toxic bacterium – but, if closed down, results in job losses? What does an ethical analysis propose?

Corporations have influence in government with lobbyists attempting to influence legislators, for good or ill, to act according to the interests of the lobbyists and their companies. Does a lobbyist have a responsibility to be truthful or just to represent his/her company's interests? Christian ethics comes down on the side of truthfulness – and its consequences – but that will probably be considered naïve. Issues can become exceedingly complex – but it is the responsibility of the ethicist to uncover hidden agendas, separate out and uncover the issues, and attempt to find reasonable solutions that will benefit the entire community rather than the narrow interests of the company.

Corporate Executive Compensation

Executives of large companies are often compensated in millions of dollars annually, in salary, bonuses, deferred compensation, stock awards, retirement pay and other benefits (including severance pay) – far greater than the employees who do the major share of the work of the company. One could ask if their compensation is justified by the value they bring to the company, to its workers and customers, and to the community at large. If an engineer at a company, with major responsibility for product reliability, earns X dollars, is it justifiable for the Executive to be compensated at a level 20 to 40 times that level – or even more? Executives must make important decisions that affect everyone. Sometimes they do well. At other times, they do not do well – but can still be compensated at extraordinary levels.

So, what should an ethical position be concerning just (i.e. rightful) compensation for people who lead a company, manage its employees, determine a value product and are responsible to the owners (i.e. shareholders)? It could be a big responsibility but it's a responsibility in relation to the other employees who contribute valuable services to the company – and the public it serves. Shouldn't the executive compensation be related in some way to the compensation of the other employees? One approach should be to make the compensation of the executive a multiple (e.g. 10x or even 20x) the *average* compensation of all of the company's other employees – or some other meaningful approach – rather than leaving it open ended, where the sky's the limit. Should government in some way enforce that limit – or should it be left to the company itself?

In sum, there is no justification for unlimited compensation in an equitable society.

What does the wealth gap do?

According to Wikipedia, "The net worth of U.S. households and non-profit organizations was $94.7 trillion in the first quarter of 2017, a record level both in nominal terms and purchasing power parity. Divided equally among 124 million U.S. households, this would be $760,000 per family. However, the bottom 50% of families, representing 62 million households, average $11,000 net worth.

In January 2014, media reported that the top wealthiest 1% possess 40% of the nation's wealth; the bottom 80% own 7%. Similarly, but later, the media reported, the "richest one percent in the United States now own more additional income than the bottom 90 percent".[7] The gap between the top 10% and the middle class is over 1,000%; that increases another 1,000% for the top 1%. The average employee "needs to work more than a month to earn what the CEO earns in one hour." Although different from income inequality, the two are related. In *Inequality for All*—a 2013 documentary with Robert Reich in which he argued that income inequality is the defining issue for the United States—Reich states that 95% of economic gains went to the top 1% net worth (HNWI) since 2009 when the recovery allegedly started. More recently, in 2017, an Oxfam study found that eight rich people, six of them Americans, own as much combined wealth as half the human race. A 2011 study found that US citizens across the political spectrum dramatically underestimate the current US wealth inequality and would prefer a far more egalitarian distribution of wealth.

From the perspective of Christian ethics, the question is whether this enormous disparity can be tolerated in a just society. What it means is that we are developing two societies: one for the rich and another for the rest of people. What it means is that wealth, converted into political power, can dominate, at the expense of the rest of society. Wealth can buy elected officials, either through electoral campaigns or through office holding (legislative voting) and, in turn, public policy. The poorer ninety-nine percent are rendered powerless.

Christian ethics suggests that citizen equality means freedom for all, the ability to live life on an egalitarian basis without domination by anyone over another – a just society, free of want or deprivation. Such a society, of course, has never existed – nor will it ever exist. Nonetheless, despite being an unattainable goal, it is an ethical objective for which we should strive.

Data Collection, Spying & Secrecy

During World War II, there were spies who sought out valuable information in the U.S. to send to their Axis governments in an effort to weaken the U.S. engagement. Were they entitled to gain secret government information? Were they entitled to transmit that information to another government? It was wartime and the intent of these spies was to gain military advantage over the U.S. – and the effort to do this was military in nature and severely punished when the spies were caught.

Today, we are confronted with issues involving disclosure of information via the Internet that is personal (private) as well as business and governmental. The Internet has made such intrusion and dissemination of information feasible and possible. What governmental information, in fact, is justifiably held as Secret and what should be disclosed? Is Wikileaks a justifiable public service or a traitorous disclosure of information that is properly held close to the vest? The Freedom of Information Act attempted to answer that question. From an ethical perspective, it is a conversation that should continue.

Personal information, however, is a separate matter. To what extent does government – and anyone – have the right to obtain personal information about you that you do not want discovered or disclosed? To what extent does the Christian ethic relate to the issue of personal privacy? – or of government intrusion into one's personal information? There is no doubt that these are difficult ethical issues – but they are issues that, in this complex, modern age must be considered.

The matter of personal privacy is a human rights issue, the right to privacy against those who would intrude and make personal information public. One position would be that a person has the right to keep personal information – age, marital status, race, sexual orientation, political identification, sources of income, personal philosophy, place of residence, nationality, etc. a private matter should he/she wish. In a practical sense, it is nearly impossible not to make such information available, if only to one's government. But, what about one's communications to someone else? Who has the right to see your e-mail, sent over the Internet?

What Christian ethics seems to say is that your personhood – your humanity – should not be violated by another party seeking to do you harm, even embarrassment, nor should one person seek to do that to another. Everyone is entitled to their privacy and any effort to do harm to another could not be justified.

Government Misbehavior

It is fashionable to denigrate government and contemptuously castigate government officials for ineptness, misbehavior, inefficiency, laziness, and an uncaring attitude, if not for outright dishonesty and fraud. In any bureaucracy, private or public, you will have instances of such behavior. But, that misrepresents that vast majority of government workers who take their jobs seriously and strive to do the best they can for the people they are sworn to serve. It is the role of the Christian to support that ethic, to encourage government workers and to expect them to live up to the high standard expected of them.

It has been contended in some political rhetoric that "Government is the problem". But, that is only occasionally true. Government exists to be the solver of problems. The Christian ethic for government is to support it in its service to the people. No one should slip through the cracks. In our modern-day, remarkably complex society, only the government has the resources to support its people, whether it be in housing, food safety, health care, education, protection from violence, transportation, civil rights enforcement, commerce, cyber security, neighborhood protection, policing, environmental pollution and protection, etc. It is appropriate that Christians encourage a civilized and safe society. But, where government discriminates unfairly and fails in its responsibility, it is also appropriate for Christians to expose, criticize and do what they can to rectify such behavior. Where government officials act perversely for their own benefit, or by showing favoritism, it is the responsibility of Christians to act against them. Where falsifying information occurs, it is the responsibility of Christians to expose the truth.

Education, Teachers & their Union

Encouraging people to think independently was clearly an objective Jesus had in mind for his disciples and listeners. It was the reason he taught in parables, encouraging people to think about his teaching. It's obvious that, as a boy, he attended synagogue school for he was apparently well versed in the Law and in Jewish history. His commitment to education reflected his desire that people think about their values and understand the meaning of life.

In Jesus' day, the education of the child was carried on in the synagogue or, in the Greek world, in the local academy. In Palestine, the rabbis or priests were the teachers and religious teaching was imbedded in the course of study. In fact, throughout the Middle Ages, education was the responsibility of the church.

That emphasis on education has carried on over the centuries, a mission embraced by the Christian church, whatever its divisions, whatever its other faults. True, the church did not always encourage independent thinking, but it did carry through on the impulse to learn. The first arrivals in America from Europe established schools and centers of learning and many colleges owe their existence to their church founders.

A Christian ethic supports education as a mark of self-fulfillment and self-realization. Education, of course, is far ranging and today includes not only the traditional liberal arts but the more objective arenas of medicine, the social sciences as well as the natural sciences, mathematics, engineering, biology chemistry, astronomy, as well as the new technologies, including even artificial intelligence and space engineering.

There has been a substantial controversy lately over the course of action concerning the education of children. The ultimate goal of education is to enable children to grow into mature adults with the ability to think independently and with strong capabilities and good judgment that will benefit not only themselves but people and society in general. This requires a good education system, good schools and good teachers. Examining their local public school system, some parents decide that their child can get a better education in a private, parochial or charter school – or even by being home schooled - than in the public school system. That, of course, is their right – and there is a cost for choosing to do it that way. The question, then, is whether the public system, no longer having the responsibility for the child's education, should cover at least part of the cost of the child being educated elsewhere.

The mode of education should be a primary concern for Christian ethics and the people who embrace an ethical perspective. There are no simple answers to the questions posed by the responsibility of educating children and maintaining a need to learn throughout our lives. What is important is that we keep the need to educate out in front of us as we proceed through life. That is a primary role for the church.

Jobs vs. Environmental Pollution

The Keystone XL Pipeline and the Dakota Access Pipeline controversies, as well as pipeline ruptures and oil spills that have occurred, have brought into sharp relief the issue of jobs and oil/gas delivery versus the threat of environmental pollution. Given the recent breaks that have resulted in pollution of streams, rivers and landscapes, the possibility of a pipeline break cannot be completely discounted. On the other hand, completion of these pipelines will result in the creation of employment for workers during construction as well as thereafter. What, again, is the ethical stance of the Christian with respect to these controversies? What is the appropriate stance of the Christian with respect to impact of a project on the environment versus the opportunity for job creation?

While the environmental impact could be long-lasting and have serious consequences, the need for employment is likely urgent but temporary — as well as short-lived. Is the measurement of these consequences relevant to a settlement of the question? These are the issues — and they pose an important consideration.

Some thoughts: In periods of low unemployment, there are usually jobs to be found somewhere, although different jobs provide different levels of compensation. During times of high unemployment, jobs are scarce, and one is fortunate to secure employment. However, protecting and preserving the environment is important for now as well as extending into the future. Considering that the environment has already been despoiled by human occupation of the land, it becomes ever more important to preserve and protect what is left.

The ethical approach to the situation would probably be to try to find a middle ground that seeks a solution, attempting to satisfy each objective without providing complete satisfaction. The objective would be to obtain the cooperation of both advocates, each recognizing the validity of the other's objective. The least important consideration should be the excess profit motive.

CHILDREN

Child Welfare

How we regard our children can make all the difference in how they develop and grow. There is no doubt that parents and other adults can strongly influence how they mature and grow into adulthood. Parents serve as role models for children and, for better or worse, will almost certainly affect what kind of adult the child becomes. An authoritarian parent can cause a child to adopt an authoritarian lifestyle and become a little tyrant, even if he/she distances him/herself from the disliked parent. An understanding and supportive parent can influence the child to be helpful and supportive to others.

The appropriate goal in raising a child is to enable him/her to become self-reliant, capable of positive achievement and helpful to others. Other children may not have the love and support they need to become the adults they need to become so it is the role of other adults to do their best to fulfill the missing role. Churches have played a role in children's lives in helping them to become mature, self-confident adults.

Adoption

The adoption of needy and orphaned children is a badly needed practice – if done for the benefit of the child and done in the right way. Those who will help children in this way are to be commended. Adoption is certainly an expression of the Christian ethic to care for one another.

But, where adoption is done for economic advantage or for abusive reasons, it is not to be allowed or tolerated. It can only be done for the benefit of the child. But, the issue becomes clouded with other questions, such as family priority or racial and ethnicity questions. Should a white American family be allowed to adopt an African-American child – or a Russian child? Should a Native-American couple be allowed to adopt a white child? What about a Catholic family adopting a child born of Jewish parents? Should a gay couple be given parental rights to a child born to a parent who disdains homosexuality? These are difficult questions to resolve – and courts often decide in ways that seem unfair or improper. If Christian ethics are applied to these cases, would they be decided differently – and should they be?

Again, no hard and fast rules apply, except that the best interests of the child should be paramount, while simultaneously considering the concerns of the adults for the welfare of the child. There are situations where judgments must be made that are exceedingly difficult. Legal decisions are not always the best and should defer to ethical judgments.

Sexual Exploitation of Children

Situations occasionally arise (but more commonly than is generally thought) where a child is sexually abused by an adult, even by a parent. Such situations may be more frequent than is commonly thought. It is amazing how many adults confess to being sexually abused as a child. Such experiences are predatory on the mind of a child and can do lasting psychological harm to a person. Sexual abuse of children has even been perpetrated by clergy and church leaders, although it is incongruous how anyone can reconcile his/her ethical responsibility as a religious leader with such behavior.

It should be expected that members of the Christian community should take notice of such behavior and seek to respond properly when it occurs. Covering up, hiding or excusing such behavior is inconsistent with one's ethical responsibility. At the same time, allegations of sexual misbehavior can be long-lasting for the accused and should not be made lightly or irresponsibly. Children need to be protected from perpetrators – and properly treated when misbehavior occurs.

As noted already, technology over the last 250 years has created the need for decisions that just didn't exist in earlier years – and the pace of technology and the complex ethical issues surrounding technological development are huge and difficult. Environmental issues are profoundly greater than earlier inasmuch as the consequences of those decisions are much longer lasting than when it was simply a biodegradable world. It was never before thought that the world had limits of sustainability and that human impacts could be devastating and long lasting.

But, from an ethical perspective, humans have been regarded as stewards of the world and responsible for its maintenance. The Garden of Eden story in Genesis emphasizes that point.

Global Warming

It is not a question in serious dispute about the rapid warming of the climate over the past century, evidenced by the melting of the polar ice caps, the changing weather and the statistical record. The evidence for the human impact on the atmosphere is indicated by the rapid increase of CO2 and methane over the past century. So, the question of global warming caused by human activity, supported by an army of scientists, is hardly in doubt. The real question is what, if anything, is to be done about it. It's an ethical question that's important for the Christian community to address, informed by scientific findings, as difficult as they are to prescribe. It's not an irrelevant issue for the concerned Christian, since the lives of everyone are at stake. Everyone should be involved in the discussion and the debate.

Every person on the face of the earth leaves a carbon footprint. Each of us impacts the environment by contributing to the CO_2 overload. Each has a responsibility for minimizing his/her contribution to the impact. An important topic for discussion in the church is: What can I, as an individual, do to minimize my carbon imprint and reduce my contribution to global warming.

Nuclear Power

The discovery of nuclear fission opened up the opportunity for the generation of energy without the consumption of fossil fuels, an environmentally favorable development. Nuclear power plants have been constructed but there have been problems. The Chernobyl reactor overheated and spewed radioactive material across the Ukrainian landscape for miles around, resulting in the evacuation of residents in the vicinity. The Diablo Canyon reactor (San Obispo County, California) was built on an earthquake fault and eventually dismantled and abandoned. The Fukushima disaster in Japan, caused by a tsunami, also resulted in the destruction and evacuation of a huge coastal area. The disposal of spent fuel rods, that remain radioactive for thousands of years, is a problem that has not yet been resolved. And yet, were these problems to be solved, nuclear power is an otherwise clean, efficient, and economical way to generate the power needed for a heavily populated world. Its proponents claim that it will solve our need for energy in an environmentally acceptable way.

It's a question that Christian ethicists can and will debate for decades to come – if not longer: how best to serve human needs without causing harm to present and future generations.

Pollution

In Jesus' time, pollution was probably not a serious problem and certainly not one that caused much comment or controversy. Most garbage was biodegradable and degraded away. Towns and villages had garbage disposal dumps that kept garbage away from homes and dwellings. Sewage gutters were probably the most significant problem and could have been the source of diseases such as cholera – but the relationship of sewage to disease was not understood. Sewage was likely controlled due to the smell. As a result, pollution was not considered the important issue that it is currently.

What makes pollution a controversial issue today is its relationship to the economy and jobs. There is a cost to controlling the pollution that affects ground water and the air that we breathe. It can translate into a company's profitability as well as to the jobs that can be affected. The control of emissions into the atmosphere costs money. Prevent a chemical plant or a coal company from dumping tailings into a stream – and it costs money to devise an alternative disposal process. Require a pipeline being built to circumvent an environmentally important waterway and it becomes more expensive. Prevent an environmentally destructive factory from being built and it costs jobs. So, what is more important: money, jobs or the environment? From an ethical point of view, what is the answer?

When President Obama issued air pollution regulations for coal-fired power plants that would cost companies substantial amounts of money to rectify, there were howls of protest, claiming the regulations were costly and would be ineffective. Subsequently, President Trump lifted many of these regulations, resulting in further air pollution. Is there an issue of ethics here that Christians should take seriously? No doubt, issues such as this are complex and require some detailed knowledge that most people don't have. So, on which side should someone who takes ethics seriously come down? How important is expert knowledge – to what extent should it guide the decisions we make? Who has the burden of proof?

Where there is a situation that could be negatively affected by a proposed change, isn't it important that the proponent be able to show that either the action will not worsen existing conditions, that the possible change is justified by the result, or that the adverse condition can be contained? Otherwise, the Christian ethicist must reject the proposed change.

The issue is not unlike that of mine safety. In years past, mine tragedies were a fairly common occurrence, resulting in hard fought battles to require installation of safety features to prevent cave ins and explosions. Such tragedies are less frequent today but do occur, as happened in the Upper Big Branch Mine in West Virginia in 2010, where the company sacrificed safety regulations for profits, resulting in an explosion that killed 29 miners.

In the modern world, there are means of protecting people from harm that did not exist even a hundred years ago. The air pollution in cities like Beijing and New Delhi could be mitigated, if not eliminated, by inhibiting traffic and shutting down coal-fired power plants. Those measures would be costly and would entail much public objection. So, there is a trade-off between risk and economic security. It's not easy to grapple with these issues – but thoughtful people who take their ethical (Christian) responsibility seriously need to strive to work out reasonable answers.

TECHNOLOGY

Technology itself poses ethical issues that are essentially new, although two hundred and fifty years ago, Luddites in England reacted against industrial development, based on their fears of how factory work affected people's lives, removing them from work on the land. Today, technology allows people to interact with machines (viz. the Internet and Alexa) rather than with one another. People are being displaced in their work by robots. The implications of technological development are so great that it is a mistake to ignore how they impact our lives. The ethical impact is a matter that churches should take seriously and about which they should host discussion. There are ethicist resources who could help.

DRUGS

Drug Policy

Most countries have segregated drugs into several categories: (1) those that are legal over the counter, (2) those that are legal with a prescription from a physician, and (3) those that are illegal (known as street drugs). The ethics of drug use is an entirely separate matter and independent of their legality. Drugs can be helpful to the body's natural functions, they can be neutral, or they can be harmful (in a variety of ways). Some are non-addictive while others are addictive in varying degrees. Because they affect one's personality and behavior, addictive drugs can have an indirect effect on other people who come into contact with the user.

For the most part, people demand and use street drugs because of their mind-altering capabilities. This requires an illegal import network, a distribution network, and a local vendor network. Because of competition, it leads to bribery, fraud, theft and violence. Attempts by local authorities to outlaw and curtail drug trafficking have only been partially successful.

From an ethical standpoint, the use of drugs can be evaluated on the basis of their effects on the user and their indirect effects on others. Because they are illegal but still are demanded by their market, street drugs create their own underground market and are a source of illegal, and sometimes violent, crime. Societies outlaw these street drugs on the basis of their disruptive impact on society.

The drug user, especially the user of addictive drugs. Is putting his/ her life at risk and yielding to an addictive problem, losing control of one's life. The Apostle Paul offered an important insight into humanity when he noted that "you are God's temple and God's spirit dwells in you" (I Cor. 3:16). One doesn't need to be theistic in order to understand that the price to pay can be severe for relinquishing one's independence and judgment to a foreign substance. Nonetheless, addiction to drugs is not necessarily an issue of choice or decision – since addiction is hardly voluntary. Once hooked, addiction becomes a health issue and needs to be treated as such.

There's hardly an ethical issue related to the use of drugs that lie outside of the remedial health issue. There's hardly a case that can be made to justify the use of addictive, mind-altering drugs not used for pain relief or for other health reasons. The question for the Christian ethicist is to understand and respond adequately to the addict and user, to limit his/her impact on others, and to minimize the impact of drug use - -especially illegal drug use – on society.

Marijuana

The issue over marijuana in American society is its legalization, particularly its medical use for pain relief and other treatment. Marijuana is a mind-altering drug, although its effects are relatively mild – but it has also shown itself to be effective in pain relief and for other treatment of mental and physiological conditions. In some states, it has been approved for recreational use. There is dispute over its addictiveness but, like alcohol, it has been cited as a contribution cause of crime and traffic accidents when use has been abusive.

Christian ethics is permissive to some extent and has long ignored the use and consequences of marijuana use. While tending to discourage its use for recreational purposes., it is unlikely to want to encourage its use, apart from its medical benefits. What is a responsible and ethical position concerning marijuana? It's a good subject for debate.

SEXUAL ORIENTATION & CIVIL RIGHTS

Issues relating to sex are controversial in most societies, with death being the sentence for transgressions in some societies, even today. Why sex should almost universally be the focal point of one's morality is probably attributable to the intimacy involved and issues of identity, trust and betrayal. One cannot be more intimate with another than through the sex act - but the betrayal of that relationship can also be understood as the ultimate act of rejection. From that reality, the moral code evolved.

Marriage

Marriage is a cultural phenomenon, not a religiously prescribed condition. It is a culturally defined union of (usually) two people to live together and to bear and care for children. There is no marriage ceremony or particular blessing that is noted in the Old Testament. Men simply took wives who bore them children. Most of the patriarchs (Abraham, Isaac, Jacob et.al.) had more than one wife. David and Solomon had multiple wives and concubines. Eventually polygamy died out, but not because it was proscribed by God. It was a cultural phenomenon. On the one hand, it served as a survival benefit for women – though it also became an economic burden for most men. But, even today, wealthy men in the Middle East are found to have several wives, without any religious (whether Islamic or Judaic) prohibition of the practice. Where monogamy is the cultural norm, it is embedded in the law.

What IS a desirable characteristic of marriage, supported by the Christian church's interpretation of marriage, is the nature of the relationship, based on the writings of Paul, the love and respect of each partner for the other and the mutual responsibility of lovingly nurturing the children who are in their care. It is not a servitude relationship of one for the other, not a condition of dominance of one over the other, not a contest of power.

LBGT Issues

In mainstream society in most cultures, it is taken for granted and established as the norm that men are attracted to women and women to men. But, that is not always the case. Whether genetically prescribed or socially induced, some people are attracted to others of the same sex – or even of both sexes. This is the case across all cultures, even though some are more punitive of homosexuality than others. Today, in more than seventy countries, same sex relationships are illegal – and in a few, such relationships are punishable by death. For those who find themselves attracted to others of the same sex, that reality can be the cause of great anxiety, so much so that suicides among homosexuals and bisexuals are not uncommon.

Ancient Greece aside, homosexuality has been proscribed in most cultures throughout most of historical memory. The Old Testament Book of Leviticus condemns it as deserving death, along with adultery. It is only recently in the Western world that homosexuality – gay and lesbian – has been socially tolerated and even accepted. Most "evangelical" churches remain outside the circle that includes gay and lesbian people as welcome within their congregations, despite instances in which a few pastors have been found to engage in homosexual relationships.

Gay Marriage

Gay (homosexual) couples have lived together quietly for many years – in the United States, Europe and elsewhere without much attention being paid to their relationships. Society assumed that people were just sharing living space and made no assumptions that they might be engaged in a sexual arrangement. It was only at the end of the 20th century that gay couples began to claim recognition for who they were – and to declare it with acknowledgement and pride. No longer feeling they needed to hide the true nature of their relationship, gay couples began to feel that they deserved the right to marry – and the legal rights that attended to marriage - that society accorded to heterosexual couples. It was at that point that the church's position was addressed - and challenged – since the church commonly performed the marriage ceremony.

This has not been an easy problem for the churches to reckon with. Some have refused to consider the issue and have used the Biblical proscriptions (in Leviticus) to support their position. Other churches have been willing to engage in the discussion in a more flexible way and to listen to those who argue the marriage claim. A book by Mark Achtemeier *The Church's YES to Same Sex Marriage* is among those arguments that make the case for understanding and acceptance of same sex relationships and the blessing of the church for same-sex unions. Several denominations have now permitted and authorized same-sex marriages within their churches. Some individual congregations have severed their denominational ties over this issue and even established denominational structures that eschew these relationships and marriages.

After centuries of following the inclination of the culture to eschew – if not persecute – homosexuality, some churches are willing to look with understanding about the plight of these people who have been pilloried by society. Accepting them for who and what they are seems to accord with the demeanor of Jesus toward the outcast and ostracized. The forces that seem to expect people to change their identity are more consistently in line with the authoritarian mold of hardline bigots than with the understanding and reconciling compassion of Jesus.

From an ethical point of view, it seems more appropriate to regard people with an attitude of understanding and tolerance and acceptance than with a more judgmental one of disgust and condemnation. Given the few Biblical citations that condemn homosexuality (Leviticus 20:13, I Corinthians 6:9) *, it has been a difficult journey for the church – and for Christians – to come to a more accepting understanding of people who identify themselves as homosexual – and who seek to live in loving relationships with another person of the same sex and who find themselves raising children together. They have endured ridicule, hostility and ostracism because of the long-standing attitude of society – but they have courageously endured. They have raised well-balanced children who have chosen their own path through life. Society has changed – and will continue to change – and there will be less discord because of it.

[* The Old Testament's harsh judgment in Leviticus 20 against sexual relations between prohibited parties, neighbors, in-laws, beasts, men, etc., merits death or ostracism, providing punishments which, fortunately, are no longer followed, even among Orthodox Jews. Note that even innocent women who are the victims of the act are to receive harsh punishment. The ethical judgment on such acts has evolved since the early time when such punishments were deemed necessary to maintain order within the group. Paul's view in his letter to the Corinthians, hundreds of years after Leviticus, was to equate theft and homosexuality with greed and drunkenness. Again, modern understanding of these conditions has evolved. Paul was reflecting the social understanding of his day, two thousand years ago.]

Again, what is important is the nature of the relationship between the two participants in the marriage. There is nothing to prevent such a loving and caring relationship between two people of the same gender. There is nothing to say that those people could not adequately and lovingly nurture a child (or children) as sufficient parents. There is only a prejudicial culture that could make such a relationship a problem.

Transgender Issues

Only in the latter part of the 20th century have we become aware of transgender issues, that the sex of a person could be other than male or female, that people born with the sex organs of one sex could actually identify as being of another sex and want to live life in that way. There even occur, in rare instances, people whose sex organs are ambiguous. Only more recently has medical technology been able to help people change their sexual identity. It is a cruel joke of nature that people have been born with these confusing characteristics that cause so much grief and anxiety. Society has made life even more miserable with its lack of understanding and acceptance.

Following in the footsteps of Jesus who seemed to accept people as they find themselves, even the confused and humiliated, the Christian ethic proposes that it is a character trait of the Christian to do the same, to be supportive and helpful to those who are burdened by such unusual and difficult identity characteristics.

RELIGIOUS FREEDOM

The Role of Religion in American Society

There has been no constant as far as the importance of religion has been in America. Certainly, early migrations to America were the result of religious persecutions in Europe, for the most part of Protestants fleeing Catholic antagonisms in central Europe. But, it also worked in reverse, as Catholics sought refuge in Maryland and other places due to the antagonism of Protestants in various parts of Europe. The early settlers in New England were Puritans escaping the hostility of Anglicans in England. Once in America, immigrants tended to congregate around their European origin churches though this was not uniformly the case. Especially on the frontier, people seemed to lose identity with their home religion and became more independent.

For those who had been settled for decades in America, deism became popular, as it was among many of those who engaged in the political life of the country, late in the 18th century. Unitarianism flourished in New England while the Anglican church gravitated to less reliance on doctrine and more on its historic ritual. Religion withered on the frontier until, early in the 19th century, a Great Awakening occurred, revitalizing evangelical fervor. Religion has waxed and waned over the intervening years, its fervor being sectionally and class differentiated.

There has been an ongoing argument over whether the United States is a "Christian nation" and whether the Founding Fathers meet the criterion of having held orthodox beliefs. Clearly, there has never been a religious test to qualify for one's civil rights or citizenship. The Constitution guarantees religious freedom, meaning that one is free to choose his/her own religious affiliation – or none at all – and that no religious prescriptions can be adopted by any lawmaking body. With the *Hobby Lobby* decision by the Supreme Court in 2014, the question at issue is just how much freedom a citizen operating a business can exercise in discriminating against a customer on the basis of religious belief. Can I, for example, as a state-licensed electrician, refuse to install lights in a butcher shop on the basis of my religious belief that contends it is unethical to slaughter livestock?

American history is replete with religious observances. School classes would begin with a recitation of the Lord's Prayer. Public meetings would begin with prayer, usually given by a Protestant clergyman. Christmastime creches would be found on the lawns of city halls and state capitols. God was invoked to obtain victory at the beginning of a military raid. All of this occurred despite the Constitutional provision against the "establishment of religion". The authors of the Constitution had concluded that the European background experience had been too painful to have it prolonged or repeated. Thus, they decided that no religious perspective could be given any preference or priority.

Still, there are those who contend that the United States, as a "Christian nation", allows the posting of religiously-related slogans, Bible verses and tableaus on public property – while others argue vociferously that doing so is a violation of the Constitution. There are some who argue against the exemption of churches and religious institutions from paying taxes – and against public support of chaplaincy services as well as the offering of prayer before the start of public meetings. What justifies having a chaplain for the U.S. House of Representatives in Washington, paid for by the taxpayers?

A Christian ethic seeks to be fair to all parties concerned, to provide every person with equal treatment before the law, to insure the independent right of every person to his/her own ideas and beliefs, to guarantee the right to think freely. A Christian ethic refuses to denigrate or discriminate against others for characteristics that don't matter. It was Jesus who asked his followers to be servants to others, not hostile business owners.

FOREIGN AFFAIRS

Foreign Relations

The Christian has a different perspective on foreign relations than is common in the body politic. "America first" has been heard periodically as a political slogan. Prior to the Second World War, as fascists were marching across Europe and threatening Great Britain, it was used as a slogan intended to prevent the United States from coming to the aid of the forces opposing fascism. In the campaign of 2016, it was again used as a code phrase for America to withdraw from the global stage.

"America first" not only proposes an isolationist strategy, it raises the ethical question asked of Jesus: "Who is my neighbor?" It suggests that Americans care only about themselves, that other peoples and nations merit indifference and that nations and peoples need not care about the welfare of others. The Christian ethic of shared responsibility for the welfare of all mankind is irrelevant to the 'America first" crowd. Fortunately, it has been embraced sufficiently in the 20th century that the United Nations supports agencies that provide relief to refugees, children and those afflicted with famine and disease outbreaks in various places around the globe. In the wake of the World War II disaster, the world, through the UN, recognizes the responsibility we have for one another.

Where the idea of mutual responsibility gets trickier and more complicated is where political systems are involved. What does global responsibility require when tyrannical regimes deprive their people of the freedoms we have come to expect and take for granted in the democratic countries of the West? On occasion, we have resorted to war to overthrow those regimes, generally with disastrous results: North Korea, Vietnam & Cambodia, Afghanistan, Iraq, The U.S. has not only sacrificed many of its military combatants in these engagements, the citizens of those countries have also suffered, resulting in many causalities and civilian deaths. So, if the U.S. is better advised not to engage militarily but feels a responsibility, nonetheless, to attempt to secure relief and justice for the beleaguered, persecuted and oppressed people of these countries oppressed with tyrannical regimes, is there an ethical strategy to pursue? That's the issue Christians are commanded to grapple with – finding an effective but humane solution to a difficult and complex problem.

Dictators & Dictatorial Regimes: Dictatorships and Democracy are completely incompatible.

When Adolf Hitler became the dictator of Germany in 1933, he was not the first national leader to assume complete power over the people of his country. History is replete with those who have claimed and exercised absolute power. Because Hitler exercised Nazi control over most of Europe for a few brief years, he is likely regarded as the most severe and overarching dictator of past recorded history, the last three thousand years. No one is responsible for so many deaths as Adolf Hitler.

Historically, Jews have been persecuted by dominating forces. In the early years of the Christian era, Christians became the target of royal vengeance. During the Middle Ages, it was heretics and non-believers who were persecuted by both church and civil authorities, wielding dictatorial powers. Some hid, some recanted, but some defied the authorities – and paid with their lives. So, what is the proper response to dictators and those wielding dictatorial powers?

Throughout the course of history, Christians have found that their only recourse to resist dictators – even at risk of their own lives - was to do what they could do to protect and shelter those who were targeted for persecution or even death. Dictatorships demand loyalty – absolute loyalty – based on the dictator's contention that he (universally male) is absolutely sovereign over the lives of his people. Christians, who have espoused freedom of the individual before God, have denied the sovereignty of the dictator and insisted that rulers are subject to the will of the people – and to a definable ethical regime.

Foreign Needs & Domestic Needs

There is a tendency to call one's own country superior to others in basic character and privilege, as suggested in the "America First" slogan that crops up at various times. A government certainly has a priority responsibility to its own people – but needs also to recognize that it has a responsibility for the welfare of everyone throughout the world. While it may be just to demonize the government of a country, it is not justifiable to demonize its people. Supporting the people of South Sudan, people who are being victimized and starved, is just as important as supporting the people of South Carolina, though the means to do so are more limited. Bombing the citizens of Yemen or Afghanistan is just as reprehensible as bombing the people of New York.

Christian ethics calls for a universal respect for all countries and people, for continued efforts toward reconciliation where there is distrust, strife and hostility. Whether it is Canada and Mexico, Great Britain and Japan, Russia and North Korea, the effort must be to seek eventual accommodation and friendship, all within the context of universal justice.

Israel & Palestine

The conflict between Israel and the Palestinians has gone on since 1947, for at least seventy years – and shows no signs of ever ending. As the stronger and more viable entity, Israel holds the keys to settlement – but, despite coming close, has failed to do so. Christians regard Jesus Christ as the Agent of Reconciliation. The Apostle Paul calls for Christians to be Reconcilers and to break down walls of hostility. Nonetheless, in the land where Jesus walked, there seems to be little hope for reconciliation, even though we have seen programs that bring together Jews and Muslims from each side of the border dividing Israel from the West Bank - to build friendships.

It seems so easy to bring hostilities to an end. Let the Jews cease the settlements in the West Bank and allow the Muslims to establish East Jerusalem as their capital. Encourage the Palestinians to recognize Israel and cease their hostile activities. Shake hands and agree to live peacefully together. But it doesn't happen. Wounds are too deep and hostility too ingrained for either side to give. American Presidents have tried in succession to bring the parties together – and on occasion, have almost succeeded.

But, don't give up. Christians have a responsibility to continue to encourage reconciliation. Don't take sides. Just keep the parties talking and working together to build relationships and draw closer together. Don't place blame when one draws back. Just continue to encourage. Show what the benefits of reconciliation could be. Make it happen.

ISIL – Syria & Iraq

In the wake of the American government's disastrous venture into Iraq in the first decade of the 21st century, a new, hostile entity was born, the Islamic State in the Levant – or Daesh (commonly called ISIS or ISIL). Violent, vindictive, murderous, destructive, the Islamic State declared itself a Caliphate and swore to make its rule known throughout the Middle East, if not the entire world. They successfully recruited new fighters from many countries around the world. Its soldiers murdered Christians as well as those they consider heretic Muslims. They destroyed cultural treasures of the ancient past. Frustrated in its efforts by American-supported forces in Iraq and Syria, Daesh has relinquished its territory and seen its leadership annihilated - and is in substantial retreat. But, will it completely disappear - forever? Will it resurface at some point in the days and years ahead?

The idea of an Islamic state is not new and will probably never disappear, even though there are numerous Muslim-dominated countries. ISIS is committed to a violent, terrorist ideology as a means of moving its agenda forward. Most Muslims regard the Islamic state idea as disharmonious, if not heretical, and want nothing to do with it. But, every religion (including Christianity) seems to have its anti-social radicals – and Islam is no exception. Daesh's fury is directed as much toward Shiites and other Muslims even more than it is toward Christians. Even in these days of ISIS' waning power and influence, there will still be those who cling to the aspirational goal of Islamic dominance. Those who do not cooperate and agree must die.

Daesh has no regard for any life or artifact of civilization unless it conforms to Daesh's narrow concept of what is acceptable. It is ultimately a nihilistic, anti-social, destructive philosophy, not even a religion. It claims to be the true Islam, but it fails to be true to the generally accepted norms of Islam. Most Muslim clerics reject and decry its claims to be the true interpretation of Islam.

Christian communities in the Middle East have been victimized by Daesh with many people killed. So, how are Christians throughout the world to regard Daesh and its adherents? In a violent military confrontation, people have no recourse other than to resist. But, if adherents are separated from the milieu of ISIS, they can be regarded as individuals and dealt with as people who have been misled and potentially redeemed from a nihilistic approach to life. The goal of the Christian is for people to be recovered and restored rather than to be forever condemned for their mistakes.

What gives one hope is that there are those who have been attracted to Daesh but then, when seeing the terrible violence that Daesh perpetrates, flee from Daesh and return to the civilized world, repenting of their foolhardiness. The message that Christians can take to Daesh fighters and adherents is that there is meaningful life apart from the tyrannical destructiveness and hopeless martyrdom of Daesh, that acknowledging the humanity and worth of others is far better than coercing and murdering them, that an affirmative approach to life is superior to the nihilism of a false interpretation of Islam.

ARE CHRISTIANS TOO SOFT?

The reality is that, as individuals, we can only do so much. It's a matter of time, energy and other obligations. But, together, we can manage to do much more. The Christian church is present everywhere in the world today, even in countries that are hostile to it, even in the Muslim countries of the Middle East. In countries like the United States, it is not only tolerated, it is welcomed and embraced. The controversy is over whether it should be acknowledged politically. There are arguments over whether Christmas crèches should be displayed on public property, whether the Ten Commandments should be displayed in courthouses, whether prayers should be on the agenda at public inaugurations, and, fundamentally, whether the United States is a "Christian" nation.

People seem to have forgotten their history, the Inquisition and the religious persecutions that occupied Europe throughout the second millennium. Many people fled Europe for the North American continent to escape the persecution that took place there over those centuries. Seeking to worship as they wished, they came to America. Peculiarly, in some colonies, they only sought to enforce the new orthodoxy. It was an innovation when Roger Williams led his Baptist followers to Rhode Island to establish a new colony that welcomed all, regardless of religious profession.

Fortunately, the idea took hold. By the time of the American Revolution and its aftermath, it was obvious that the establishment of a religious orthodoxy was counterproductive to the America that was coveted by so many – so any establishment of religion was prohibited by the Constitution. Were it not so, the United States would just become another battleground for religious discord, persecution and rebellion. Still, there are those today who campaign to bring back an establishment of religion – their religion.

Is that the role of the Christian church today – to encourage the establishment of the Christian religion? That's hardly what Jesus sought to do – or would seek to do. Remember, he was rather contemptuous of the political and religious authorities of his day. His interest was in healing, justice, righteousness and compassion. He despised hypocrisy, insensitivity and selfishness.

So, what is the role of the church today? Is it to escape from the world in closeted church services, to gloss over the things that are important and unjust and offer its adherents a place to hide in comfort? St. Paul offers some idea when he suggests that the Christian community is to engage in a "ministry of reconciliation" (2 Cor. 5:19) in the world. Now, that's an interesting commission, to bring people together in a world of understanding, trust and commitment to one another.

During the 20th century, numerous service clubs (e.g. Rotary, Kiwanis, Lions, Optimists, etc.) have sprung up to develop projects to benefit their local communities and even foreign communities. Some have rather minimal objectives (such as building bus shelters) but others have serious and significant goals such as constructing clean water projects in African villages, playing fields for the handicapped, microcredit projects to enable women to start homegrown industries throughout the world, establishing food banks and homeless shelters in the U.S. and elsewhere, and providing medical equipment for remote places in South America. While churches support foreign missions, they tend to be less numerous and have less impact that the service projects of these international service clubs. Nonetheless, service clubs and organizations likely owe their inspiration for such projects to the example and ethic of the churches, mosques and synagogues in earlier America.

Suppose the church were to define its primary role as Jesus did: to preach release to the captives (those deprived of their political rights), the recovering of sight to the blind (those who obscure the truth), to set at liberty those who are oppressed (Matt. 25:18)? What a revolution that would be! The church of the future must take seriously its responsibility to be an agent of reconciliation in the world.

14

CHURCH PRACTICE TODAY

THE IMPORTANCE OF THE CHURCH

The fact that many Americans attend church regularly makes it clear that participating in congregational life is important for these people, whether for social, psychological or other reasons. People want a place to belong and socialize with others. Churches have provided that place to congregate (with like-minded folk & those who share the same social characteristics) and the theology of that church has been, for the most part, incidental. (When have you last heard arguments in church, even from the pulpit, over the theological issues that one divided Presbyterians, Lutherans, Methodists, Baptists, Episcopalians and others?) Today, there are many other institutions and organizations that provide the social benefits that churches once exclusively provided, Nonetheless, churches aren't going away even though some congregations may wither while others flourish. Throughout American history, that has been the case. Participation in church life has fluctuated.

In recent years, "evangelical" churches have seemed to be the strong attractants, even though "evangelical" religion seems to be on the wane. What has attracted people to these churches has been its emphasis on contemporary music, often a digression from popular country music, and the variety of activities being sponsored, from child care to sports activities., from various arts to Bible study. Mainline churches have been less creative in this way but more engaged in community service activities. Mainline churches have also been more willing to accommodate commonly accepted scientific and social information.

Without churches, communities would be less cohesive and resilient. But, the existence of churches leaves much to be desired, if only in the intellectual arena. Being stalwart advocates of truth-telling, churches should be in the forefront of education as they once were, and centers where ideas – especially ethical and political ideas - can be shared. Too many churches are not open to criticism for their inadequacies and challenges.

THE ROLE OF RELIGION IN A DEMOCRRATIC SOCIETY

America was a religiously pluralistic society from the very beginning. Even Native Americans represented a variety of beliefs and ceremonies before the arrival of the Europeans. The arrival of Spaniards introduced Catholicism into Florida, California and the Southwest. English Puritans introduced their own brand of Anglicanism which diverged into Congregationalism, the Baptist spinoffs and eventually Unitarianism. The Dutch around New York introduced the Reformed churches and the Scotch brought in Calvinism (Presbyterianism). When Germans arrived in Pennsylvania, they carried a variety of traditions, including the Mennonite, the German Reformed, the Moravian and the Lutheran. The Scandinavians, coming into the Northwest, were primarily Lutherans. Southern Europeans (Italians, French, Germans), arriving through Ellis Island, were predominantly Catholic.

This melting pot of religious beliefs and traditions could only be accommodated by a tolerance and advocacy of religious freedom, at the time known nowhere else in the world. Nonetheless, churches were quite distinct in their doctrinal and theological differences and held to their distinctive traditions into the early 20th century. Such doctrines as Baptism (Submersion vs. Christening), Predestination, the Virgin Birth, glossolalia (speaking in tongues), Biblical inerrancy, et al were hotly disputed and supplemented by distinctions over church governance and ritualistic practices. For the most past, political issues were ignored.

THE ROLE OF THE CHURCH TODAY IN THE CONTEMPORARY WORLD

With few exceptions, the church prefers to avoid controversial social and political issues – and the arguments that go along with them. And, yet, it's hard to see how the church can have any relevance or importance without confronting those controversies that pose moral and ethical issues. Shouldn't the church be the place where those controversies are discussed and even argued over – with the message and personhood of Jesus as the reference point? The church's mission is to get at the truth ("The truth shall make you free.") and then to act on the basis of compassion ("Love one another, even as I have loved you.").

But, it is not so simple. As Pilate said to Jesus: "What is truth?" It is one thing to ignore the truth. It is another to try to define the truth since it is often not clear. Pilate might also have said: "What is right – or Righteousness?" These virtues are not always easy to define. It is one thing to give a beggar a dollar. It is another to do so and to guard against the abuse or ill-use of that handout.

That is why Christians need to be in constant conversation with one another – to sort out Truth and Righteousness and to act with real compassion. In the preceding chapters, we have discussed the multiple, contemporary issues that cry out for discussion within the halls of the church. It is important that this discussion take place within the context of mutual respect – and that there be understanding of the opposite point of view, even though one side seems to be more "compassionate" than the other.

.BUILDING A MEANINGFUL AND SIGNIFICANT CHURCH

It is in the realm of ethics that the church could play a significant and meaningful role by bringing people of different backgrounds and viewpoints together. By considering and identifying various issues discussed above, churches could make a major contribution to society. Whether it's discussions about abortion or the rehabilitation of lawbreakers or a responsible foreign policy, churches can encourage people to consider various viewpoints in the light of ethical criteria.

Throughout history, given populations of people have been characterized by a gradient of knowledge, intelligence, thought and consideration of ethics. People have arrived at varying conclusions over issues and occupied varying positions, some after much consideration, some with little. But, humans are characterized by their intelligence and their ability to think. The more they display these characteristics, the more responsible their conclusions, even though their conclusions may differ. What is important is that they engage in dialogue – with respect for one another. The church needs to be the facilitator of that dialogue.

BUILDING A SUCCESSFUL CHURCH

Successful churches are not always acting as responsible institutions in their communities. A church that promotes an anti-evolution conference is not being a responsible presence – nor is a church that foments anti-gay rhetoric or that leads demonstrations against a woman's right to choose. Truly successful churches are those that deal responsibly with information, that eschew ignorance and bigotry, that find a role in serving the needs that exist in the community as well as in the wider world and that involve their participants in important issues and meaningful activity.

THE ROLE OF THE PASTOR TODAY

For starters, let's get our terminology straight. "Reverend" is an adjective, not a noun. The Rev. Mr. Evans is grammatically correct, and Rev. Evans is acceptable. "The Reverend went...." Is not correct and is not acceptable. Reverend is not a noun. On the other hand, Rabbi is a noun as well as an adjective – and so is Father (for a Catholic priest). A person who is ordained is Clergy. A Clergyperson who serves a church is a Pastor – or a Minister. A clergyperson who is not serving a church but who is working in another occupation can be called a cleric, clergy or Clergyperson. A Clergyperson teaching at the college level is simply referred to as Professor – or even just Mr./Ms. (or Dr.) Evans.

The Pastor – or minister – right off the bat faces a dilemma: role identity. Is he – or she – primarily an orator (preacher), an administrator, an educator, a counselor, a therapist, an advisor, a healer, a peacemaker and reconciler, a fund raiser, a prophet, a leader, an information resource, a Biblical/theology authority or a cipher for another? Deciding on one's primary function is critical – but challenging. And, are the pastor's employers – whether Board, Elders, Bishops, Consistories, etc., clued in and in agreement with the role the pastor has chosen for himself/herself?

The Pastor can be a great catalyst for the creation of a thriving community of those who are committed to its mission.

Another dilemma a Pastor must deal with has to do with changes in his/her thoughts or beliefs as time passes. It's true for all of us. Experience not only changes us but causes our knowledge, thoughts and beliefs to change. We are not the same at 20, 40 or 60 as we mature and age. For Pastors who make certain creedal affirmations when they are ordained, it is hard to turn back and revisit that occupational decision. As they grow older, their beliefs evolve and they are no longer committed to the same beliefs. Yet, many find themselves occupationally chained to the orthodoxy they championed when younger. It is very sad to see clergy in their later years have no alternative than to continue to espouse views they no longer embrace They neither serve themselves well nor serve their congregations well. The liberated Pastor can shape and decide who he/she wants to be as Pastor. He/She can define the role to be played.

But, the Pastor faces another dilemma: the role he/she wants to play vs. the role he/she is expected to play by the congregation. These alternative roles can be widely divergent and the source of conflict.

And, then, there are the many functions the Pastor can be expected to perform. It' rare that any one person could perform all of these functions well. And, yet, here are the usual expectations of the Pastor:

1. The Pastor should be counselor to those in need.
2. The Pastor should be Preacher.
3. The Pastor should be a Guide to the congregation in fulfilling its role.
4. The Pastor should be an Educator and Biblical scholar.
5. The Pastor should be a Community Organizer.
6. The Pastor should be an Administrator.
7. The Pastor should be a Therapist.
8. The Pastor should be an Advisor.
9. The Pastor should be a Healer.
10. The Pastor should be a Reconciler and Peacemaker.
11. The Pastor should be a Prophet.
12. The Pastor should be humble.

That's a huge diversity of functions to fulfill. Pastors who are introverts would do well to find another profession. Even Pastors who are extremely smart and capable will need to be selective about the role and functions that he/she can perform well.

CHURCH MEMBERSHIP

One becomes a church member by acknowledging certain statements of faith, usually after attending a communicants' class where some of the doctrines of the Christian faith are presented and discussed. It's hard to imagine that the communicant is doing anything more than agreeing with some creedal statements that are unsupported by any fact or that involve a real and vital commitment to do anything more significant than to attend church services on occasion and recite a creed when there. What of importance is involved?

So, why do people attend church? Is it because there is something there of importance other than to commingle and visit with other churchgoers? Is Sunday camaraderie the reason people show up? Is worship the real reason they come?

Let's acknowledge that people attend church in order to participate in a friendly community, i.e. for social reasons. Let's acknowledge that some of those people find the Christian message significant and important in their lives. But, there are others for whom the creedal statements and the message of faith are not important but that they come primarily for the social benefits. There are some who participate because they want to be part of a community that does good works and they want to participate in a "Christian" mission. Perhaps they could still be participants and officers of the church but not be subject to reciting creedal statements that are meaningless to them. Perhaps there could be two categories of church membership: (1) the creedal communicants and (2) the community members. Both would have rights of governance, but only creedal communicants would have authority over the denominational connections of the church and its theology.

PRAYER & MEDITATION

Prayer has been part of the human experience from time immemorial. It was originally supplicatory, requesting the gods or God to change His/Her mind or at least intervene and grant the request. It might be for one's self – or for someone else – or for a changed condition and is usually preceded by a statement of praise and thanksgiving.

When Jesus asked the disciples to pray as he taught them, it is interesting that there is no statement of thanksgiving in the prayer (although, on multiple other occasions, Jesus did offer thanks to God). It opens with an address to the Father, a request for the coming of the Kingdom, and a hope that God's will shall be done on earth, that is, that good things will happen. There is then a request that one's daily food be forthcoming. Then there is the hope that we will not be more judgmental than we ourselves are judged by others ("Forgive us our trespasses as we forgive others"). Pitfalls and mistakes are many and the prayer asks that they be avoided ("Lead us not into temptation'"). The final phrase of praise was added later and was apparently not part of Jesus' original prayer. It is certainly a brief prayer and not overly concerned with imploring God to change the course of events apart from one's own physical necessities ("Give us this day our daily bread.") and the righteousness of one's inner being ("Deliver us from evil"). It is a prayer that seeks to make the human life be characterized by goodness towards others. Note that it has nothing to do with one's salvation or changing the will of God or the course of events.

In primitive and pre-modern societies, it was common to ask God to change things, to give victory in battle, to rescue one from sickness, discomfort or horrific events, to render the impossible possible. Today, we ask God to heal the sick, even to cure sickness, to restore the abused and oppressed, to bring soldiers back from war unscathed, to prevent accidents. So, what are we trying to do? To get God to pay attention to our particular concerns? To change His/Her mind? What is prayer for?

Prayer is more likely thought of as meditation – to rectify one's mind and emotions. Prayer is more likely properly focused on the needs of others as well as our need to be faithful servants and to live meaningful lives. In praying, we are expressing our concerns, the things that trouble us, the people we need to keep in our thoughts, the best possible outcomes of bad situations. Prayerful meditation is attending to our own selves in the context of our spiritual vocation rather than asking God to pay attention or change His/Her will.

SONGS & HYMNS

Music has been a part of Christian devotional services from the very beginning of the church in the first century. Congregations today sing songs and hymns that date from the Middle Ages up to the present.

Some have sentimental words (e.g. In the Garden) while others are militaristic (e.g. Battle Hymn of the Republic). Some are meditative (e.g. Blest Be The Tie That Binds), some theological (e.g. The Church's One Foundation), some celebratory (e.g. Joyful, Joyful, We Adore Thee). Some familiar music from years past has now been accorded contemporary words. The lyrics convey meaning and are important, though often overlooked or ignored. Amazing Grace is an example of a beautifully moving song with theologically questionable lyrics, even though written by a wicked, wretched man whose life had been turned around by a religious experience. Joyful, Joyful We Adore Three (Beethoven's Ode to Joy) is one of the most joyful and uplifting – and theologically acceptable - songs in the Christian hymnal.

Some hymnals now provide explanatory notes at the bottom of the page. Congregants seldom read these, though they are explanatory and help the understanding of the hymn. Perhaps, a song leader could read these notes before the congregation sings the hymn.

WORSHIP

In the manner of the early Christian church gatherings, the worship service should be simplified and less focused on the supernatural and creedal and should emphasize the mission and challenges ahead. In Acts, those who considered themselves followers of Jesus would gather to sing and reflect on Jesus who had brought them together, perhaps with some Scripture (Old Testament & Epistles) readings, perhaps with some discussion about how they should relate to one another and to others around them, perhaps even with respect for how they should go about their daily lives. For these early Christians, worship was a time to renew themselves, to gather strength and to focus on living in the world.

Gradually, there developed a few who spoke more frequently and became known as the teachers and preachers in the congregation. Ritualistic forms developed, and more formality characterized gatherings of Christians. Theological issues were discussed, and an orthodoxy developed, especially in the churches aligned with Rome and Constantinople. Other congregations with less orthodox views were censured and even excluded from the main fold. Yet, all were Christians and were dedicated to following the teachings of Jesus.

What emerged from this was a gradual theologizing and spiritualizing of Jesus and less focus on the kind of life that he taught his followers to lead. Many of the arguments that developed were not centered on the societal responsibilities of Christians but on the nature of God and the personhood of Jesus, rather esoteric issues that were, in the context of what Jesus taught, not really important.

So, how could worship be modified in order to be more focused on Jesus' teaching and the lives of the worshippers? Periodically, through the ages, there have been attempts to recapture the spirit of the early church. Perhaps, most notably, the Quakers have attempted to worship as they are moved by the Spirit. Some groups have excised singing, some have forbidden musical instruments. But, these are irrelevancies.

Worship is a time of reflection and renewal. It should be a time of coming together, to experience a sense of community, to reflect on mission and communal responsibility, to discuss issues and opportunities in a context of ethical responsibilities. It should be an opportunity to transcend the ordinary. As such, it makes sense to be exposed to musical and artistic expressions, to foster the creative, to share one's concerns, to ponder difficult problems. to hear a variety of thoughts.

Worship should not be structured any more than necessary, though some structure is required in order to allow for all of these things to happen. Perhaps it could be structured as follows:

> Musical Prelude
> Welcome & Peace as a greeting
> Congregational Song
> Events of the Past Week
> Crises
> Notes from other Christian communities
> Choral Music
> Old Testament Reading & Remarks
> Congregational Song

Shortcomings & Meditation
Reading from the Gospels and Remarks
Anthem
Reading from the Epistles and Remarks
Pastoral Remarks and Conversation
Unison Statement of Commitment
Offertory
The Lord's Meal - Sharing
Looking forward to the Days Ahead
Congregational Song
Charge & Benediction

The congregation should be invited to express their own thoughts about Biblical passages and the issues and theme for the week, much as the Quakers are accustomed to doing. The pastor can lead the discussion without dominating it, while keeping it on track and focused on the theme for the week.

CREEDS & CONFESSIONS: THE CONFSSION OF THE CHURCH THROUGH THE AGES

The Nicene Creed is one of the earliest dogmatic confessions of the church developed in a church council in the city of Nicaea (About 60 miles SE of Istanbul) in 325 A.D. to define Christian orthodoxy. The Apostles' Creed is of a later date – but all doctrinal Creeds were adopted to settle some dispute within the church, usually revolving about the nature of Jesus, the Christ. Some of these disputes over the nature of Jesus Christ were bitterly and violently fought. Murder was occasionally used to silence opponents.

The problem with a formal creedal statement is that it is used politically to maintain an orthodoxy which may, or may not, make sense to the individual adherent. There is no way to objectively establish its validity and those who disagree with its particulars are banned from participation in the community, even though they may wish to be part of it as followers of Jesus. It used to be a mantra of religion (perhaps it still is) that "you must have faith. You must believe" as though believing without evidence is honorable. If one believes something just because the crowd or the institution says it's true (or might makes right), then there is no standard of truth and one can believe whatever one is told to believe or to believe whatever one chooses. Arbitrariness becomes a virtue and the truth becomes a victim.

In the present day, creedal statements are increasingly irrelevant to the issues and challenges at hand. How does it matter to anything of importance today whether Jesus was conceived by the Holy Ghost, rose again from the dead and sits at the right hand of the Father? How does it matter that Jesus was "fully human, fully divine"? Does it matter that Jesus was giving insight into what is moral behavior and ethical conduct, into how we should relate to one another and engage in relationships that are defined as just? Of course. It is THAT dialog that we should be engaged in, thinking about and acting upon.

CONFESSION OF SIN

Sit in church on Sunday morning and you are invited to participate in the "Confession of sin", however it is printed in the bulletin. Some confessions are beautifully written; some are rather trite. All are intended to help us recognize our frailty before the majesty of God. And some are intended to impose upon us our unworthiness and degradation. At the same time, on the basis of modern psychology, we know that it is mentally unhealthy for us to denigrate ourselves, to belittle ourselves, to think of ourselves as worthless. To do so can lead us to psychological trauma and even thoughts of suicide.

Assuming you are a worthy member of your community and participate in events that contribute to the lives of other people and contribute money to worthy causes, of what relevance is a "Confession of Sin"? If we take our lead from Jesus' words in the Lord's Prayer, we ask forgiveness for our transgressions against others – whether intentionally or via neglect) and that we not be led into temptation – and be delivered from evil. Those are appropriate confessions and requests – for we have all at some point committed acts that are harmful to others, have all thought about doing things that would be hurtful to others, been tempted to commit acts that would injure others and done thoughtless and stupid things.

A Calvinist approach to life would render our lives worthless and God as the omnipotent ruler of all, choosing some for glory and consigning others to perdition, regardless of the nature of our lives. There would be no justice for a good and generous life and no just punishment for a Hitler or Napoleon. So, what would be the point of a Confession of Sin?

The sin is in how we treat others, as referenced in the Lord's Prayer – but the good is also in how we treat others. We are not worthless creatures but people who choose constantly to do predominantly good things for others. And, when we do otherwise, we have failed our own purposes and destinies. A Confession of Sin simply makes us think of ourselves in ways that are of no value to us and to our purpose.

THE SERMON

If the sermon ever had any useful place in an edifying service, it is long past its time. Most sermons seem to be irrelevant to the lives of the people They are one-way communication – and their content tends to blow over people's heads. "Good sermon" may mean that the preacher's words were interesting to listen to – but they do not engage, they do not involve, they do not challenge the listener to think differently about a relevant subject, they do not change people's lives.

There were times in the history of the Christian church when people argued over meaningful issues – because they considered them to be important. That is hardly the case today. Do parishioners talk about the content of a sermon with respect to how it affects their thinking and their lives? What people argue about are the conditions in town, about the people around them who confront them, about the social problems that exist in their communities – or that threaten their communities.

These are the things that people care about: zoning, crime, miscreants in the community, labor, taxes, honesty and competence among officials, insensitivity to their needs, their personal health, convenience and inconvenience, government actions, other needs of the community, unfamiliar people, sports and other forms of entertainment, etc.

In order for words to have any effect, one needs to be involved with the content, to be conversant with it, for it to be relevant to their lives. Perhaps religious monologues are entertaining but rarely are they relevant. Perhaps they are interesting, but rarely do they inform in any way that matters. Perhaps they stir the emotions, but rarely do they provide meaningful insight. There needs to be something more – and actually the church has a potentially important role to play in making those few minutes on Sunday morning worthwhile.

So, let's try this. Make the pastor's role one of selecting the topic and the relevant Bible material – and introducing the issues involved. Then let four or five other people - lay people from the congregation – express their thoughts about the material presented. Let there be a conversation leaving the opportunity for others in the congregation to ask questions and express opinions. Create a meaningful conversation among everyone present with the objective of causing everyone to consider their own thoughts about the subject and to carry on the conversation with themselves and others through the week. Churches should experiment with this idea and seek to have everyone engaged in thoughtful dialect.

Uniformity of opinion is not the objective – but to challenge people to think about important issues – to heighten the awareness of people to issues of significance and to enable them to converse with others, even with others with whom they disagree – but all committed to responding to an image of Jesus of Nazareth and dedicated to finding an approach to an issue they believe Jesus would take.

BAPTISM & COMMUNION

In the Protestant churches, there are historically only two Sacraments: Baptism and Holy Communion, whereas the Roman Catholic church observes seven Sacraments. A Sacrament is an observance of an important event, a special occasion in which a momentous act in the Christian life takes place.

If we are to demythologize our religious practice, we are inclined to deemphasize these Sacraments but that does not mean that we should abandon them altogether. Baptism is the welcoming of a child or person into the community of fellowship, a dedication of the person to following Jesus and a commitment of the people of the congregation to provide for the nurture of that person. The practice need not be abandoned.

The Lord's Supper is a reminder of who we are as a people, a people who have dedicated themselves to following Jesus, even to the point of sacrifice. As it is currently observed, it is more than that. It is intended as a mystical union of the person with that of Christ, a transcendent act. In practice, it is carried out with a great variety of intentions on the part of communicants. Some take it very seriously, some do it casually or even frivolously. But, what it is - is a meal in which Christian people gather together to share a meal, a fellowship in the spirit of Jesus, a reminder of our responsibilities to one another and to the world at large. It would be prudent to make it that and to dissolve the mystical aspects of Holy Communion. By institutionalizing and making it sanctimonious, we downplay the sharing and communal aspects of the Lord's Supper.

CHRISTIAN EDUCATION – YOUTH & ADULTS

So, what is it that the church should teach? Most of us are familiar with the traditional Sunday School in which we learned about the Garden of Eden and the Tower of Babel, about the faith of Abraham and the devotion of Isaac, about Joseph and Moses and Samson and

David – and about the life of Jesus. It was mostly Bible stories with little memorable point. There wasn't a lot about making ethical decisions. Yet, that's what it's all about.

You can attend church as often as possible, you can say your prayers regularly, you can read the Bible faithfully, but the proof of the pudding is how you live your life. Jesus was constantly calling people to task for their carelessness, their insensitivity and their hypocrisy. He wanted people to be attentive to and responsive to one another. He was constantly battling greed and the accumulation of wealth and encouraging people to abandon the valuation of things and look more assiduously at "spiritual" and human values. If there is a purpose to be served in Christian Education, it is to encourage awareness of the decisions we make and the things we value. Even with small children, we can initiate a discussion of values and decision-making in the context of Christian love and values.

THE SUMMER CAMP EXPERIENCE

Summer camp can be a wonderful experience for children and families. It is a marvelous opportunity for education in a context of freedom and openness. Unfortunately, there are some camp leaders who think it is an occasion to evangelize campers, making it a time of guilt and intimidation.

CHURCH GOVERNANCE

As far as we know. Jesus never envisioned the formation of an institution centered on himself. He gathered a group of disciples who followed him on his wanderings around Palestine, a group who made various attempts to spread his story and his values following the Crucifixion. We don't know much about any of them, even Peter whose efforts were eclipsed by those of Paul who wasn't even a disciple. In any case, it was Paul who founded church communities throughout the Greek world and launched what would become the Christian church. If it had been left to Peter and the other disciples, it is unlikely that the Christian congregations would have survived.

However, they did survive and grew and became more institutionalized as time progressed into the second, third and fourth centuries. With Constantine and the state recognition of Christianity, the church emerged above ground and its hierarchy became well established and accepted. As it grew, it became more like other religions with its emphasis on relics, dogmas, icons and meeting structures. After a period in which various bishops competed for leadership, the bishop of Rome emerged as the primary head of the church in the west. Over the centuries, with varying degrees of success, the Papacy attempted to exert civil and political authority as well.

The institutionalization of the church, however, led to some very unfortunate consequences which led the church in directions that were actually hostile to the message of Jesus. Whereas Jesus had been critical of the Temple hierarchy and the affluence of the Temple officials, the church gradually developed its own system of powers and adornments and influences which were contrary to Jesus' message bringing relief to the poor and oppressed. Whereas Jesus had little interest in dogmas and orthodoxy, the church sought to punish those who did not adhere to its dogmas. Whereas Jesus opposed bigotry (viz. the Good Samaritan), the church sought to persecute those who failed to conform to its definition of a "good Christian" and who challenged its authority. It even, on occasion, endorsed slavery, misogyny, and racism. It developed close ties with the powerful and trod upon the poor.

THE ARTS

Without the church, the world of the arts would not have progressed as rapidly and notably as it did. The music of the church, its frescoes, paintings and sculptures – even its architecture - are evidence of its major contribution to the humanistic arts. It would be a much poorer world without these contributions to aesthetic appreciation and human understanding.

Even though support for the arts has largely been usurped by the secular world, the church has a role in continuing to make a contribution to the arts.

THE CHURCH & MONEY

Churches are faced with a substantial dilemma with respect to money: it must compete with other organizations that are established to accomplish certain humanitarian and do-good objectives. Churches usually exist with staff costs, building costs, supply and maintenance costs, etc. and may have little left over for aid and services for the poor and needy, civil rights, environmental safety and other causes. Yet, it is the latter that should arguably have priority.

Church members who take their Christian commitment seriously have the same dilemma: how to allocate the dollars they have available to donate to various causes, including the church. Everyone needs to make these decisions among those appeals for financial support, appeals that seem to be endless.

There is, of course, no general answer to this problem. However, churches could open up the discussion for how people should think of their charitable donations – rather than merely occupying a competitive position. Where will dollars be best used? What are your individual priorities? Should Doctors Without Borders be juxtaposed with the local campaign for establishing a National Wilderness? Should your local hospital be prioritized over a U.S. Senate campaign? These are important choices that require thought and discussion. Perhaps the church is where this discussion could help.

15

CHURCH CELEBRATIONS

There is no reason to abandon the church year. The occasions that occur during the year are opportunities to remind us of various facets of social injustice and needed action that must be attended to, lest they be overlooked or forgotten. As Paul reminded us, there are many roles to play in the mission of following Jesus. No one can play them all – but it is helpful to be reminded of the overarching mission that the church has entrusted to it – and to be sure that needs are being attended to by someone in the church. The events and celebrations of the church year are enumerated below, with suggestions for areas where attention could be given. See if they apply and could make the year more meaningful and productive.

ADVENT THEME – CHILDBIRTH & ABORTION

In American society, commercial interests begin using Christmas as a marketing device immediately following Halloween, even though Advent, the season in the church year preparing for Christmas, doesn't begin until after Thanksgiving. More than fifty years ago, Christians protested that Christ was being taken out of Christmas. Whether Christmas was ever a religious holiday, it is true that, over the years,

Christmas has been increasingly secularized, so much so, that even Jewish families feel forced to acknowledge it with gifts to their children.

The period of Advent is, according to the church model, a time of preparation for Christmas. But, what does that mean or imply for modern Christians of the 21st century? Society has deemed it a time for charity fundraising, largely motivated by potential deductions from one's tax return. Still, whatever the motivation, Advent is an opportunity to make a meaningful contribution to whatever cause one values.

But, Advent can be an opportunity to do more than that. It is an occasion to reevaluate what one's role is in society and to consider how your contribution can be enhanced with a restatement of your priorities. It's a time for the church to reconsider its role in the community and what its contribution should and could be. It's a time for mutual reflection and soul searching, not merely for decorating the church in festive décor, but for real inclusion and response to the needs of the outside community and the people within it.

Advent can be used by the church for the discussion of the implications of bringing children into the family, involving both the joy and hardships involved, including the assumption of a new responsibility. Using the model of Joseph and Mary, the church can reflect on what it means to bring a new person into the family, how that person shall be regarded and nurtured, and how life within the family will be changed. Even the question of whether it is the responsible thing to do to complete a pregnancy could be discussed with consideration of whether abortion would be the more responsible course to pursue.

CHRISTMAS THEME – RELIGIOUS FREEDOM & THE ROLE OF A RELIGIOUS ORIENTATION

We celebrate the birth of Jesus of Nazareth on this day, even though we have no idea when he was born. Even the mythology contained in the Gospels is hard to accept because of the differences between them. The genealogies are different between Matthew and Luke and contain material such as the Annunciation and the Magnificat that would be hard for anyone else to know. The birth narrative in Mark, the first Gospel to be written down, is absent and the writer of John's Gospel also doesn't seem to know the story.

Nonetheless, the Christmas story is a part of our culture and it would be hard to dismiss it. So, what can we learn from it and be edified by it without sentimentalizing it? Obviously, Joseph and Mary were a poor couple in need of shelter for the birth of their son, at the time of the census supposedly called by Augustus Caesar, although there is confusion about the coincidence with the reign of Herod, who died in 4 A.D. What is clear is that Jesus was born into a condition of injustice, evidenced by the occupation of Roman legions and the surrogate rulership of the puppet Herodians. The Jews of Palestine were seriously oppressed, a condition that continues in much of the world today. Jesus came to set the prisoners free – yet the exploitation of people continues.

The commemoration of Christmas by the church should concentrate on the relief of suffering by the poor and oppressed. There are approximately 20 million refugees in foreign countries and 65 million total displaced persons in the world today. Finding ways to relieve poverty and misfortune would be the most appropriate way to observe Christmas. This is not merely a one-day activity to provide a meal and perhaps a few presents for children but the beginning of a campaign to discover the structural conditions that create poverty and homelessness and the beginning of a change in those structures so that poverty might be eliminated from the local scene and people might be enabled to live meaningful and opportunistic lives.

Christmas, then, is an occasion for discussion and action to relieve the conditions that oppress the unfortunate – and to create those conditions that will support and enliven those who have lost hope and merely live to survive

Lent Theme – Civil Rights

We observe Lent as the time when Jesus came to Jerusalem and was arrested by the Roman authorities. It's not clear why he was arrested but, clearly, he was considered a threat by both civil and temple authorities. Not only was his message considered dissident, but he was apparently drawing sizeable crowds that were considered potentially troublesome, if not rebellious. He had to be stopped.

Violations of civil rights persist to the present day, where abuse of authority occurs occasionally in American and Western society and more frequently elsewhere. While racial tolerance appears to be widely practiced, the tolerance of homosexuality, gay marriage and abortion is less tolerated, in varying degrees, especially in those countries where homosexuality is outlawed and punished. Still, it is a fairly recent discovery that a significant portion of society is gay and that those people deserve and demand basic rights and acceptance of their lifestyle. One doesn't need to be gay to recognize that people deserve acceptance regardless of their sexual orientation. This is as basic a norm as a racial, religious or gender right.

Lent is a time to recognize that all people are brothers and sisters, that they deserve respect and honor to the extent that they do not intrude upon the rights of others to personhood, dignity and respect. That is the way in which Jesus dealt with others. Only those who exploited others were regarded by Jesus with contempt.

In our day, we classify the right of others to full participation in society as a civil right, deserving of a just role in society, regardless of gender, sexual orientation, race, and national origin. Is it a civil right of a pregnant woman to terminate her pregnancy?

Wouldn't it be appropriate for a church congregation to deal with this question during the period of Lent when it is appropriate to consider one's faults and inadequacies – and be observant of Jesus' message not to criticize another when the critic is guilty of even greater faults? Isn't this the time to forgive and restore?

GOOD FRIDAY THEME – THE CRIMINAL: INCARCERATION & CAPITAL PUNISHMENT

Justice is often elusive. When Jesus was crucified, it was unclear what crime he was guilty of – or even charged with. Nonetheless, he was found deserving of death and was executed in the Roman manner, by crucifixion. (The Jewish manner was by stoning.)

It's hard to conceive of anything more unjust and wrongful than punishment for a deed you did not commit, especially in a society founded on principles of justice. It leaves one feeling completely helpless and depressed. It robs a person of any hope. Justice becomes a meaningless word. One's life has been destroyed.

It is amazing how many people have been found innocent of capital crimes since DNA has been used to exonerate them of crimes for which they have been convicted. Some have been on death row awaiting execution. Others have been sentenced to life or for many years in prison. What this demonstrates, of course, is the rate at which people are wrongfully convicted for crimes of which they are not guilty. Where DNA is not available for conviction or exoneration, what is the frequency of wrongful conviction?

This is not to diminish or neglect the terror involved in serious crimes. Where someone has been assaulted or hurt or deprived of property by a deliberate act of violence or theft, punishment is called for, although within humane bounds. But, conviction and incarceration of the innocent is perhaps the worse wrong. Where imprisonment for political reasons occurs, that is unacceptable, regardless of the nature of the society or political system. It was probably political prisoners that Jesus was referring to when he described the role of good people as "setting prisoners free".

So, is there a role the church can play? Is there a role for Christians?

EASTER THEME - HEALTH

An important and focal part of Jesus' ministry was his attention to the health of the people. He cared for and cured the sick and infirm. His creative abilities were undoubtedly exaggerated over the years so much so that by the time the Gospels were written, he was credited with curing lepers and even restoring the dead to life. Nonetheless, the number of people attended to and cured is sufficient to know that Jesus paid attention to the sick and must have been remarkably effective a physician of his time.

The best Jesus could do was to travel about from one village to another and minister to the ill and needy. There were no clinics, no hospitals, no MDs, no pharmacies, no nurses, no nursing homes, no insurance. Health care was left to the individual and his/her family. Over the centuries, there was little to change that situation – until the 20th century when health care took a dramatic change for the better. The ability of physicians to diagnose and treat diseases improved dramatically, hospitals, clinics and nursing facilities developed exponentially, and pharmaceuticals were developed to treat various health conditions. With it all, nursing care improved enormously.

But, with it came a huge increase in health care costs and the availability of insurance to protect one against the costs. In Jesus' day, one lived as long as one could stay healthy. In our day, with the developments in preventive medicine and treatment of various conditions and illnesses, the probability of living a long life is vastly enhanced. Churches played a key role in the establishment of hospitals and care of the ill.

Easter is the annual occasion for celebrating the Resurrection, the triumph over death. What the disciples realized was that Jesus was still among them, even though he had been crucified. His life was so profound and powerful that they felt his presence among them in spite of his death. They could carry on and even perform his acts of healing and restoration.

Easter is a time for us also to embrace opportunities for healing and restoration. As it was with Jesus, health care is an important aspect of our Christian responsibility. But, the situation is vastly different and more complex than it was in Jesus' day. To put it simply, health care has been institutionalized and has become a major part of most expense budgets. The opportunity and responsibility for health care has been monetized. Health care has become a social responsibility rather than merely an individual or family responsibility.

But American society has been reluctant to assume this role while other countries have embraced it. The role of churches is to see that it gets done, that everyone has the opportunity for preventive care and healing and for living life to the fullest. Easter, then, is the reminder of that responsibility.

Without getting into the details of care alternatives, the church and church people must see that the maximum opportunities exist for prevention, care and recovery from illness and physical afflictions. The church can study and promote and lobby for social remedies to be sure that the hand of Jesus touches as many people as possible.

REFORMATION SUNDAY THEME – GOVERNMENT & INTERNATIONAL RELATIONS

Issues Affecting the Environment, Pollution

Protestant churches celebrate Reformation Sunday in commemoration of the occasion when the church was liberated from the authoritarian hand of the Pope, the Bishop of Rome. It was an innovative and creative moment when the doors were thrown open and the church was revitalized by free expression and a reconsideration of its role in the world. The Reformation was not intended to be the creation of a new orthodoxy. And, in fact, it was not. Out of it arose a variety of churches with varying viewpoints and practices, churches that in time developed separate associations, eventually developing into denominations. For the Reformers, Hus, Luther, Calvin, Zwingli and others, there was no intention to form new churches but to instill a desire to reform the existing church and to honor the Christian church as they understood it.

So, once again, Reformation Sunday is an occasion for reflecting on the role of the church for the opportunities and needs it seeks to fulfill. It's always an open question as to whether the church should be reformed. Assuming Jesus intended to give the church a mission, what is that mission and has the church come close to fulfilling whatever role Jesus had in mind?

The nascent church was formed within fifty years of the ministry of Jesus. It has been around for the past 2000 years. Until the reign of Constantine, it was an underground community of believers and even periodically for the next one hundred years. The institutionalization of the church took place over the next 800 years until the permanent split between the Eastern Orthodox and the Western church headquartered itself in Rome. The Western church increased its hierarchical authority over the next few centuries until the beginning of the Reformation in the early 1500s.

The various Protestant churches that developed out of the Reformation differed in the extent and type of authority they exerted over their congregations and people. Some, such as the Calvinists and Lutherans, continued in the Roman Catholic mold to exert an orthodoxy of belief and structure. Others, such as the Anabaptists and Quakers, were much more tolerant of deviants and anti-traditionalists, leaving much control to local congregations. Still, it was the beginning of a multi-faceted and tolerant approach to the form of Christianity that was expressed. There were periodic attempts at defining an orthodoxy and requiring universal recognition – but the trend was toward more diversity and tolerance, so much so that, when the U.S. Constitution was being formed, state religion was prohibited, and the right of religious freedom was enshrined.

Today, we live in a world where religious freedom is almost universally practiced and politically guaranteed. It is considered a basic human right along with freedom of speech and political expression. Yet, oppressive governments still incarcerate people for speaking freely and advocating for policies those governments consider unpatriotic and threatening. People still bully other people for their non-conformity to opposing values.

Reformation Sunday, thus, is not only a time for recognizing the right of religious freedom but for political freedom as well. It is a time to acknowledge the unjustly incarcerated prisoners, wherever they may be, and to seek their release. Several human rights organizations already exist for this purpose and have been successful in pushing toward this goal. Churches and church people could align themselves with these efforts and advocate the setting free of those who are unjustly incarcerated and punished.

And then, there is the Environment, the health of the world in which we live. Perhaps Thanksgiving is the best time of year to focus on the health of the planet and how we might successfully sustain it for future generations. We all share guilt for the poisoning of the world, whether through CO_2 emissions, manufacture and disposal of non-biodegradable materials, or the sheer use of toxic materials that pollute our land, air and water.

Until the dawn of the industrial age, this was not a significant issue. Today it is huge. The deterioration of the air we breathe, the water we drink, and our use of land is still escalating, with little promise of these trends being reversed in the near future.

Do Christian adherents and churches have a responsibility here – and can they be effective in doing anything about it – or should we sit blithely in our church pews, ignoring the greatest threat we have ever known to the ultimate survival of life on earth?

No one occasion evokes our attention to this issue. It is always with us – day by day, hour by hour, minute by minute. What we can do about it is to constantly recognize it, study it, and do our best to reverse it. If ever there was a challenge facing the church and its people, this is it. It won't go away.

Thanksgiving Theme - Indigenous Peoples & Native Americans and/ or Immigration & Human Rights

Indigenous Peoples & Native Americans

Humans have fought battles between clans and groups probably ever since they evolved, thousands of years ago. The Old Testament talks about warfare among tribes. Asian history is a record of stronger groups dominating weaker. Europeans fought among themselves throughout the Middle Ages. Native Americans fought their battles before the arrival of the Europeans.

But, as the age of discovery developed, military groups with superior weapons travelled great distances to dominate other populations they found could be exploited. As they sailed down the west coast of Africa, Europeans of various nationalities found they could defeat and exploit Africans of various tribes and cultures. Japanese invaded and dominated coastal China. The Spanish were followed by the Dutch and the English in overpowering and dominating the native peoples of America.

Whether these native people arrived on North American shores fifteen thousand years ago or more than a hundred thousand years ago, they arrived long before the Europeans. And they established well-defined communities with unique and developed cultures, cultures decimated by disease and warfare as the Europeans moved inland.

Native Americans still suffer the ravages of domination by a foreign culture. They are the descendants of the original inhabitants who benefited by their presence here. They do not want to be either patronized or victimized, but they do want to be accepted as equals in contemporary society. Perhaps churches, which once participated in the coercion of conformity, can offer support for granting self-respect and self-determination for these honorable people in our midst.

Immigration,

Although Thanksgiving is not a specifically religious holiday and is not an occasion of the church calendar, it is established as a cultural occasion to remember all those benefits for which we, as individuals and as a country, have to be thankful.

It is a cultural belief that the occasion of Thanksgiving has the Pilgrim celebration in 1623 as its origin. The celebrants were all immigrants, save for the few natives who sat with them. The immigrants from England and Holland were invited by their native neighbors. They carried no passports or entry papers, yet they were welcomed and supplied by the natives who received them. In a few years, they would reward those natives by pushing them back from their settlements and then resorted to gunfire and massacre.

So, for American Christians, Thanksgiving is a time to reflect on the matter of immigration. We have established rules for immigration and, as a society, we have become harsh in the enforcement of those rules. Our harsh or tenuous regard for illegal immigrants, even for legal immigrants who exhibit foreign characteristics, contrasts with the circumstances under which our forebears came to this country. In recognition of their responsibilities to the poor and desperate situation of their brothers and sisters, some churches have identified themselves as "sanctuary churches" and have provided food, shelter, and clothing to those in need.

There is no easy answer to the problem of immigration. It takes great courage to leave one's home and family and to venture off into a foreign land and an uncertain future. According to Matthew, the Holy Family, Joseph, Mary and Jesus, were refugees for a time in Egypt. If the Pharaoh had been like the U.S. Administration, they would have spent time in prison before being sent back to Herod. Desperate people take desperate measures. What is the responsibility of a Christian in such a situation? Is it the attitude of Jesus to provide comfort and help – or to make someone obey the letter of the law. Thanksgiving is a time for reflection on these things.

Observing Special Occasions

Many issues confront us as responsible citizens and Christians. We cannot assume knowledge and leadership on all of them. We must focus our efforts on a particular issue and rely on other committed followers to address other issues. The world is far more complex than it was in Jesus' day and crucial issues overlap one another, solutions for one problem create other problems. Priorities must be established and continuously reviewed. Even criteria are not obvious. Does acting inhumanely in one situation create other problems further on? Only in conversation with others who care can we find tentative answers. Being Christian requires communication about important matters.

For Evangelical Christians, it is rather simple: Are you saved? Do you know Jesus Christ as your personal Savior? All other matters are irrelevant and inconsequential. It doesn't matter if the earth deteriorates or if the non-Christian is abused and abandoned. What matters is your salvation, a rather self-centered goal, measured by what you put in the collection plate.

Throughout the year, the modern Christian examines his/her responsibilities in the world, just as Jesus and the prophets before him, asked of their followers.

16

BUILDING A MEANINGFUL
& SIGNIFICANT CHURCH

Christian churches have existed for nearly two thousand years and have existed with three dominant dimensions of character: religious belief, religious ritual and compassionate behavior. Now, in the twenty first century, religious belief is being challenged by scientific findings, religious ritual is being replaced by healthcare practice, but compassionate behavior remains an ethical imperative, as promulgated by Jesus. The church as a caring community has an important role to play in society by bringing people together to satisfy their social needs and to make a positive ethical contribution to the wider community. The role of the church is to stimulate activity that responds to the needs of people, many of whom are apart from the church but need its support and help.

To the extent that the church is a "community of believers", the belief that unites the people is that they have an ethical responsibility for the betterment of human life in both a psychological way as well as a material way. Jesus is a superb role model for this. In his life and his death (i.e. crucifixion), he was true to his calling to provide clear-sighted and honest vision, health and support to all of humanity.

The church establishes meaning for the lives of its members and significance for the larger community.

THE CHURCH'S IRRELEVANCE IN THE 21ST CENTURY

The post-war period in the 1950s was the high point for church attendance in America. Most American families, whether in the cities or in the countryside had a church affiliation and attended church at least once a month. Even singles attended church, if only to meet other singles. The churches thrived and the ecumenical movement for joint cooperation, if not union, was particularly strong.

But, in the waning years of the 20th century, participation in church activities gradually tapered down. Denominational activities and budgets were hit hard, and once-packed church congregations became thin. What had happened that churches grew weaker?

Television probably had something to do with it as it competed for attention. TV also offered a diversity of values. America became more mature with the movement for civil rights and the push for gender equality. Traditional social forms gave way. For social activities, Rotary, Lions, Soroptimists, Kiwanis, Eastern Star, Masons and others provided important contacts. Sports and recreational activities and opportunities expanded. Churches were left in the lurch as more activities competed and became available outside the church. The requirements of business activities demanded more and more time. Another element also mitigated against church involvement: the irrelevance of preaching and the social and scientific information that generated doubt of its theology. The church was increasingly seen as an anachronism.

At the same time, the traditional churches and denominations were experiencing a decline, the evangelical churches were thriving, largely with younger families. Now, as reported recently in *The Christian Century* magazine, the evangelical churches seem also to be in decline, perhaps damaged by the hypocrisy of vocal political figures who are only interested in self-aggrandizement.

THE IMPORTANCE OF THE CHURCH: BUILDING A MEANINGFUL & SIGNIFICANT CHURCH

The essential role that the church can play is to stimulate activity that responds to the needs of people, many of whom could benefit from its services and could use its support and help. The church can establish meaning for the lives of people who are seeking a fulcrum for their lives.

BUILDING A SUCCESSFUL CHURCH

In the minds of most, the Megachurch is today probably the image we hold of the most successful church, with thousands of people in attendance at Sunday services and an active program of Bible study, child care, Alcoholics Anonymous and perhaps even various sports activities. It can't be denied that such churches (usually representing a fundamentalist or conservative theology) make good contributions to their communities and to the lives of the people who participate. The question must always be asked, are they being faithful to the message of Jesus of Nazareth who sought to reconcile people to one another and called for an outreach to others outside of the local community?

We need to redefine a successful church as success in being the church, in being a reconciling and compassionate presence in the community, as well as being a prophetic voice as social critic and healer. Being a successful church is one that regularly examines itself for what it is and how meaningful its presence is in the community. A successful church is a presence that stimulates thought and provokes action.

17

GOING FORTH

THE CHURCH IN THE WORLD

Prior to the 19th century, there were few eleemosynary (charitable) institutions in the world. Care for the poor, the downtrodden, the persecuted, the oppressed was largely an individual matter. The Civil War sparked the development of organized institutions which sought to care for the wounded and homeless. In time, groups supporting women's suffrage and opposing alcohol abuse were formed. Churches began to arrange for refuges for the homeless, orphanages for children without parents, and homes for the disabled. Schools were built to train children and the illiterate and hospitals developed to care for the sick. The twentieth century saw an explosion of charitable organizations to address an even greater array of causes.

Churches and church people were largely responsible for this development. The incentive to educate, support and provide health services to impoverished people throughout the world was aroused by the desire to evangelize those whom the movement would serve. But, it also reflected a desire on the part of people with good intentions to help those in need of some form of assistance and support. Today, all of the churches carry on programs to help the needy. Christians can influence and support the efforts of secular service organizations and international NGOs such as Doctors Without Borders and Amnesty International.

Churches should continue to lead the way in showing compassion for the needy, not to convert them to some brand of Christianity but simply because Christians care about the welfare of people, particularly the poor and oppressed who are in need of help. The churches should also promote sabbaticals in which church members spend some time in a place where their help and services can be utilized.

Many kinds of project activities can be undertaken – but they should always be organized and controlled by indigenous peoples themselves. The kinds of projects are almost endless: literacy and education, schools and teachers, scholarship aid, clean water, sanitation, control and treatment of disease, health care, plastic surgery and other types of surgery, dental and vision care, medical equipment, prosthetics and wheelchairs, microcredit for small business development, agricultural projects, even transportation assistance.

The course of action, particularly when it takes a political form, is not always clear. One party wants to address a problem in a particular way, another party wants to attack it differently. We have seen this recently in the debate over health care for those who are not protected. So, where does that leave the church? Generally, the church has shied away from such controversial political subjects. Too bad. That is where the discussion should take place – in the community of those who share the common goal of resolving differences to address problems in the most efficient and effective way possible. Let the church be the center of such discussion - and be determined to find the most suitable way to move forward – even with minorities in disagreement but willing to cooperate with the majority. That's what God expects of us – and will give us the resolve to move forward.

Our purpose in life is to bear one another's burdens and to meet the needs of the poor, oppressed and downtrodden. The church can – and should be – the instrument for doing this effectively. The needs of the world are enormous. We are those who are passing by those in the world who are beaten, robbed and oppressed. We have a habit of passing by on the other side of the road, ignoring those who are in pain and distress. If we are followers of Jesus of Nazareth, we have a responsibility to minister to those needs and wounds.

18

GOD

When Jesus spoke of God, God was not a distant Being, waiting for people to accord Him the honor He coveted – or a little flame within one's inner being. For Jesus, God is the Source of our compassion and the One who expects us to act ethically on behalf of others. If the church is about anything, it is about that: being the source of compassion in the midst of the world. Worshipping God means being active on behalf of others in need.

Many years ago, Michael Novak, a Stanford professor and practicing Catholic, wrote a book titled *Belief & Unbelief*. In it, he noted that there are believers who act like believers and believers who act like unbelievers. You might conclude from that note that it's not really important that one believe in God. It's more important that you think and act as though God believes in you!

Note: Biblical quotations are from the Revised Standard Version of the Bible

APPENDICES

Appendix A – The Books of the Old Testament

Fable or Folklore

    Genesis, Joshua, Judges (could be partly historical),
Jonah (could be considered prophetic), Esther

History

    I & II Samuel, I & II Kings, I & II Chronicles, Ezra, Nehemiah

Law (Torah) & Genealogy

    Exodus, Leviticus, Numbers, Deuteronomy

Poetry & Literature

    Ruth, Job (could be considered Fable/Folklore),
Psalms, Proverbs, Ecclesiastes, Song of Solomon, Lamentations,

Prophets

    Isaiah, Jeremiah, Ezekiel, Hosea, Joel, Amos, Obadiah, Micah,
Nahum, Habakkuk, Zephaniah, Haggai, Zechariah, Malachi

Apocalyptic

    Daniel (could be considered Folklore in part)

Appendix B – The Books of the New Testament

Narrative History – The Gospels & The Book of Acts

The Pauline Epistles (Letters)
Romans, I & II Corinthians, Galatians, Ephesians, Philippians, Colossians, I & II Thessalonians

Doubtful Pauline Epistles
I & II Timothy, Titus, Philemon, Hebrews

Other Epistles
James, I & II Peter, I, II, & III John, Jude

Apocalyptic – Revelation

Appendix C – Important Dates

Moses leads the Hebrew people out of Egypt	1200 BCE
David's Reign in Jerusalem	1000 BCE –970 BCE
Solomon's Reign, The Temple Completed	970-922 BCE
The Kingdom Divided: Israel (north), Judah (south)	922 BCE
Uzziah, the King in Judah	783-742 BCE
Isaiah, the Prophet (in Judah)	742-700 BCE
Micah, the Prophet (in Judah)	?
Defeat of Israel (the Northern Kingdom) by Assyria	722-721 BCE
Exile in Assyria for Israelites	721 BCE
Jeremiah, the Prophet (in Judah)	626-605 BCE
Fall of Assyria to Babylon	612-609 BCE
Ezekiel, the Prophet (in Babylon)	593-573 BC
Defeat of Judah, Fall of Jerusalem, Babylonian Exile begins 587 BCE	
Second Isaiah, the Prophet (chapters 40-55), (in Babylon)	549 BCE
Return from Exile	c. 538 BCE
Temple Rebuilding Completed	515 BCE
Hellenistic Domination- Alexander the Great	c. 336 BCE
Ptolemaic (Egyptian) Control	285-203 BCE
Syrian Conquest	200 BCE
Maccabean Revolt against Persian rule & Hellenism	167 BCE
Judas Maccabeus	166-160 BCE
John Hyrcanus	134-104 BCE
Conquest of Shechem, the Temple in Samaria	125-128 BCE
Pompey captures Jerusalem – Roman Occupation	c. 63 BCE
Herod the Great	74 BCE – BCE
Herod Antipas	4 BCE – 39 AD
Crucifixion	c. 31 AD
Conversion of Paul	34-36 AD
Travels of Paul	c. 46-65 AD
Jewish Revolt Against Roman Occupation	67-70 AD
Destruction of the Jerusalem Temple by Romans	70 AD

Old Testament Canon formalized by Rabbinic Council of Jamnia	90 AD
Septuagint – Lain translation of Old Testament by Jewish rabbis	3rd Century
New Testament Canon formalized Constantine	313 AD
Vulgate – Latin translation of Bible by Jerome	late 4th Century
Rome-Byzantium Split	1054 AD
The Crusades	1096-1291 A.D.
Reformation – Martin Luther	1517 AD
Church of England severs from Rome under Henry VIII	1533 A.D.
Puritanism in New England	1600 AD
King James Version of the Bible published	1611 AD
Pius XI - Immaculate Conception (of Mary)	1854 AD
Papal Infallibility	1870 AD
Evolution – Darwin	1859 AD
World Council of Churches formed	1948 AD

Appendix D. Ruling Emperors, *Church Fathers*, & <u>Persecutions</u>

The Jews under the Ptolemies (Egypt)	Fourth Century BC

<u>Greek</u>

Alexander the Great	336-323 BC

<u>Persian</u>

Antiochus III	**d. 190 BC**
Seleucus IV	**187-185 BC**
Antiochus Epiphanes	175-163 BC
Profanation of the Jerusalem Temple	Dec. 167
Antiochus V	163-162
John Hyrcanus	
Judas Maccabeus	166-160 BC
Demetrius	162-150 BC
Rededication of the Temple	164 BC
(Jonathan)	160-143 BC

<u>Roman</u>

Roman Conquest	63 BC

Sadducees – drew strength from priestly aristocracy & secular nobility
        Tainted with Hellenism
      Compromise with Hasmonean priestly kings
        Roman procurator
      Feared destruction that would impact balance

Pharisees tradition of Hasidim (Maccabean) – no compromise
      Observance of the Law- Torah, Mishna, & Talmud
      Oral Law
      Clarified under Roman rule
      Chary of revolutionary activity

Julius Caesar	**46-44 B.C. (Emperor)**
Nero	64 AD Rome fire blamed on Christians

Destruction of Jerusalem Temple by Romans	70 AD
Hadrian	117-138 AD
Ignatius of Antioch, Bishop of Rome	Second Century AD
Antonius Pius	138-161 AD
Marcus Aurelius	161-180 AD
Commodus	
Septimus Severus	193-201
Lapsed in first half of 3rd century	
Revived under Maximus Therax	235-238 AD
Polycarp – first half of 3rd century	
Decius	249 AD
Gallus	251-253 AD
Valerian	253-260 AD
Respite under **Gallienus**	260 AD
Diocletian Persecution	303 AD
Constantine (Emperor)	312 AD
Julian - Paganism revived	361-365 AD
Jovian	363-364 AD

Appendix E – Herods

Herod the Great	74 B.C. to 4 B.C. Father of Antipas & Archelaus,; King of Judah at Jesus' birth.
Herod Archelaus	23 BCE to 18 AD Ruled Judea 4 BC – 6 AD when succeeded by brother Antipas
Herod Antipas	20 BCE to 39 AD. Ruled Galilee 6 AD – 30 AD; Tetrarch of Galilee; Beheaded John
Herod Agrippa	(Acts) 10 BCE to 44 AD; Son of Aristobulus IV & Berenice; nephew of Antipas

Appendix F. The Twelve Disciples

1. Simon Peter
2. Andrew, his brother
3. James, son of Zebedee
4. John, his brother
5. Philip
6. Bartholomew
7. Matthew
8. Thomas
9. James, son of Alphaeus
10. Thaddeus, (Mark, Matthew) – same as Judas, son of James (Luke)
11. Simon, the Zealot
12. Judas Iscariot

Appendix G – The Parables

The Parables:

Of Salt & Light	Mt. 5:13; Lk. 13:18-21
Of the Sower	Mt. 13:1-9; Mt. 4:1-9; Lk. 8:4-8
`` Of the Seed Growing Secretly	Mk. 4:26-29
Of the Weeds	Mt. 13:24-30
Of the Mustard Seed	Mt. 13:31-32; Mk. 4:30-32; Lk. 13:18-21
Of the Leaven	Mt. 13:33
Of the Hidden Treasure & Pearl	Mt. 13:44-46
Of the Net	Mt. 13:47-50
Of the Householder	Mt. 13:51-52
Of the Unmerciful Servant	Mt. 18:23-25
Of the Good Samaritan	Lk: 10:29-37
Of the Rich Fool	Lk. 12:13-21
Of the Great Supper	Lk. 14:15-24
Of the Lost Sheep & The Lost Coin	Lk. 15:1-10
The Prodigal Son	Lk. 15:11-32
The Unjust Steward	Lk. 16:1-12
The Rich Man & Lazarus	Lk. 16:19-31
Of the Unjust Judge	Lk. 18:1-3
Of the Pharisee & the Publican	Lk. 18:9-14
Of the Laborers in the Vineyard	Mt. 20:1-19
Of the Pounds	LK. 19:11-27
Of the Two Sons	Mt. 21:28-32
Of the Wicked Tenants	Mt. 21:33-46; Mk. 12:13-28; Lk. 20:9-19
Of the Marriage Feast	Mt. 22:1-14
Of the Fig Tree	Mt. 24:32-33; Mk. 13:28-29; Lk. 21:29-31
Of the Ten Maidens	Mt. 25:1-12
Of the Talents	Mt. 25:14-30
The Reason for Speaking in Parables	Mt. 13:10-15; Mk. 4:10-12; Lk. 8:9-10

Appendix H. The Books of the Bible & the Deuterocannon

There is no uniformity among Christian churches and traditions as to what writings constitute the Holy Bible. Variations occur in both the Old and New Testaments.

Thirty-nine books of the Old Testament are included in the Bible used by Protestants. However, this number varies among other Christian traditions, with some additional writings being included by some and some divisions or combinations among others. The Roman Catholic Bible and that used by Eastern Orthodoxy includes the Deuterocannonical books of Judith, Bel and the Dragon, Ecclesiasticus and the books of the Maccabees. But, the books of the twelve minor prophets are combined into one book as are Ezra and Nehemiah and also Ruth, Lamentations and Judges. Variations are also found in the Syrian Peshitta, the Ethiopian Orthodox "narrow" cannon and the Gregorian Orthodox Dueterocannon. Modern scholarship disputes the identity of the authors of certain writings within books, not only the accreditation of David to the Psalms attributed to him but also to some of the chapters in Isaiah, Jeremiah and others.

Protestants recognize twenty-seven books of the New Testament but variations occur here as well with Roman Catholic and Orthodox traditions. The book of Revelation was not widely accepted until the fifth century as were 2 Peter, 2 John, 3 John and Jude. Even today, scholars dispute the authorship (as well as the authenticity) or some of these writings. Martin Luther dismissed as uncanonical and uninspired the books of Hebrews, James, Jude and Revelation. The translators of the King James Version of the Bible included the apocryphal books of the New Testament in their work, though those books were later omitted.

Appendix I – Song & Hymnody

Comfort, Comfort You My People
Creator of the Stars at Night
Let All Mortal Flesh Keep Silence
Lift Up Your Heads, Ye Mighty Gates
Jesus Walked This Lonesome Valley
Wind Who Makes All Winds that Blow
Sovereign Lord of All Creation
Holy, Holy, Holy, Lord God Almighty
Come, Thou Almighty King
Come, Christians, Join to Sing
The One is Blest
Why Are Nations Raging?
Psalm 4 As Morning Dawns
O Lord, Our God, How Excellent
Lord, Our God, Thy Glorious Name
Lord, Who May Dwell Within Your House
When in the Night, I Meditate
The Heaven's Above Declare God's Praise
The Day of Need
The Lord's My Shepherd, I'll Not Want
The King of Love My Shepherd Is
My Shepherd Will Supply My Need
Psalm 23 The Lord's My Shepherd
The Earth and All Who Dwell therein
Psalm 24 Lord, To You My Soul Is Lifted
The God of Heaven
Come, Sing to God
Psalm 31: 9-16 In You Lord I Have Put My Trust
Psalm 33 Thy Mercy and Thy Truth, O Lord
Psalm 34: 9-22 Fret Not for Those Who Do Wrong Things
As Deer Long for the Streams
Psalm 42 God is Our Refuge and Our Strength
God, Our Help and Constant Refuge
Psalm 46 People, Clap Your Hands
Psalm 51 My Soul in Silence Waits for God
To Bless the Earth
Psalm 67 God of Mercy, God of Grace
Psalm 72

Appendix J – Projects for Churches

Water Supply	Clean Water	Literacy	Microcredit	Sewage
Education	Scholarships	Student Residences	Cleft Palate Surgery	
Prosthetics	Wheelchairs	Bathrooms	Home Building	Inoculations
Health Care Centers – Supplies	Medical Equipment	Boat Passage		
Books & School Supplies	Eye care/ Hearing/ Dental	Kidney Transplants		
Agricultural Training	Soy Milk			

Helping at Local Food Bank
Initiating and Supporting Microcredit Projects
Funding & Providing Wheelchairs
Providing Bikes for Children
Offering a Job Finder Service
Offering & Providing a Job Training Service
Counseling Services
Music Training/Operating a Music Band
Tutoring for Struggling Students
Language Training for Foreign Persons
Providing Child Care for Those Needing It
Pet Visitations with Seniors and the Ill
Providing a Pregnancy Clinic
Anger Control Training
Engaging a Community Chorus
Mentoring people with emotional problems
Offering an Art Class
Offering Dance Instruction
Providing After-school Activity Programs

CONTACTS (a sample)

Habitat for Humanity
322 West Lamar St.
Americus, Georgia 31709-4828
800-422-4828

Guide Dogs for the Blind
50 Los Ranchitos Rd.
San Rafael, CA. 94903
415-499-4000

Wheelchair Foundation
3820 Blackhawk Rd.
Danville, CA. 94506
877-378-3839

Wounded Warrior Project
4899 West Lamar St.
Jacksonville, Fl. 32256
877-832-6997

Peace Corps
855-855-1961
www.peacecorps.gov

Americorps
800-492-2677   202-692-1470
My.americorps.gov

FOR FURTHER READING

Belief & Unbelief	Michael Novak
Your God is Too Small	J.B. Phillips
The Forgotten Creed	Stephen J. Patterson
The Politics of Jesus	Obrey M. Hendricks, Jr.
The Politics of Jesus	John Howard Yoder
Christian Realism and Political Problems	Reinhold Niebuhr
Reinhold Niebuhr On Politics	Harry R. Davis & Robert C. Good
Forged	Bart Ehrman
Jesus Before the Gospels	Bart Ehrman
Jesus Interrupted	Bart Ehrman
Misquoting Jesus	Bart Ehrman
The Five Gospels	The Jesus Seminar, Robert W. Funk et al.
The Acts of Jesus	The Jesus Seminar, Robert W. Funk et al.

Printed in the United States
By Bookmasters